Dispatches: Turning Points in Theology and Global Crises

Dispatches draws on the legacy of early-twentieth-century theological responses to the crises of the two world wars. During World War II, the *Signposts* (Dacre Press, 1940) series sought to offer an interruption of a theological malaise in the midst of mass violence and destruction. Contributors from that series, including Julian Casserly, Eric Mascall, and Donald MacKinnon, among others, offered slim volumes that drew from diverse resources and harnessed the apocalyptic political urgency of the dialectical school within the theological grammar of a more traditional Anglo-Catholic Thomism. Similarly, and inspired significantly by MacKinnon's contributions, this present series draws on diverse theological resources in order to offer urgent responses to contemporary crises.

While the title of the series conveys the digest nature of the volumes, the subtitle, *Turning Points*, indicates the apocalyptic urgency of the issues addressed. Yet, there is no prescriptive theological stream within which the tradition is to be reappropriated by our authors. The goal of the series is to offer a genuinely creative and disruptive theological-ethical *ressourcement* for the church in the present moment. With conceptual agility and faithfulness, this series will provide intelligent and accessible reflections on the shape and form of theological life in the present.

Dispatches will illuminate and explore, creatively and concisely, the implications and relevance of theology for the global crises of late modernity. Our authors have been invited to introduce succinct and provocative arguments intended to provoke dialogue and exchange of ideas, while setting in relief the implications of theology for political and moral life.

Series Editors

Ashley John Moyse (PhD, Newcastle) is the McDonald Postdoctoral Fellow in Christian Ethics and Public Life, Christ Church, Oxford. In addition to his work with the Dispatches series, he has authored *Reading Karl Barth, Interrupting Moral Technique,* and *Transforming Biomedical Ethics* (Palgrave, 2015) and coedited several volumes, including *Correlating Sobornost: Conversations between Karl Barth and the Russian Orthodox Tradition* (Fortress, 2016), *Kenotic Ecclesiology: Select Writings of Donald M. MacKinnon* (Fortress, 2016), and *Treating the Body in Medicine and Religion: Jewish, Christian, and Islamic Perspectives* (Routledge, forthcoming).

Scott A. Kirkland (PhD, Newcastle) is the inaugural Postdoctoral Research Fellow and Research Coordinator for the Trinity College Theological School,

University of Divinity, Melbourne. He is the author of *Into the Far Country: Karl Barth and the Modern Subject* (Fortress, 2016), coauthor, with John C. McDowell, of *Eschatology* (Eerdmans, 2018), and coeditor, with Ashley John Moyse and John C. McDowell, of *Correlating Sobornost: Conversations between Karl Barth and the Russian Orthodox Tradition* (Fortress, 2016) and *Kenotic Ecclesiology: Select Writings of Donald M. MacKinnon* (Fortress, 2016).

Printed Titles

The End Is Not Yet by John W. de Gruchy

Political Orthodoxies by Cyril Hovorun

Theology and the Globalized Present by John C. McDowell

Forthcoming Titles

Gender Violence Church by Anna Mercedes

The Art of Living for a Technological Age by Ashley John Moyse

Intersectionality, Religion, and Theology by Joerg Rieger

Theology, Comedy, Politics

Theology, Comedy, Politics

Marcus Pound

Fortress Press
Minneapolis

THEOLOGY, COMEDY, POLITICS

Copyright © 2019 Fortress Press, an imprint of 1517 Media. All rights reserved. Except for brief quotations in critical articles or reviews, no part of this book may be reproduced in any manner without prior written permission from the publisher. Email copyright@1517.media or write to Permissions, Fortress Press, PO Box 1209, Minneapolis, MN 55440-1209.

Cover image: © iStock 2018; Abstract Fractal Pattern by VladNikon

Cover design: Alisha Lofgren

Print ISBN: 978-1-5064-3162-8

eBook ISBN: 978-1-5064-5835-9

The paper used in this publication meets the minimum requirements of American National Standard for Information Sciences — Permanence of Paper for Printed Library Materials, ANSI Z329.48-1984.

Manufactured in the U.S.A.

To Clare Regan
The funniest person I know

Contents

	Acknowledgments	xv
	Preface	xvii
	Introduction	1
1.	The Three Elisions of Comedy	15
2.	The Metaphysics of Comedy	67
3.	Comedy and Trinity	115
4.	Comedy and Politics	159
	Conclusion	217
	Select Bibliography	221
	Index of Names	225
	Subject Index	231

Acknowledgments

My thanks go to Sam Ford for his conversation and copy of Harvey Cox's *Feast of Fools* in the early gestation of my ideas. I would also like to acknowledge and thank Francis Stewart, who not only shared my enthusiasm for this project, his dissertation positivity contributed to the development of my thought. If I had managed more coffee with Peter Kashouris, I suspect I would have refined my thought even more. Ashley Moyse and Scott Kirkland provided the formal impetus to develop my ideas in writing. Along the way Christine Hamilton made the less-humorous tasks far more enjoyable. With Steve Ford and Dave

Haskins, the conversation was always theological (much to Dave's chagrin) and funny at once. Andy Shear and Matt Stapleton continue to be my go-to sharpening stones. Finally, my thanks to Clare Regan, a witting partner in love.

Preface

What relevance has comedy for the global crises of late modernity and the theological critique thereof? By deconstructing secular accounts of comedy, this book advances the argument that comedy not only participates in the divine but that it should inform our thinking about liturgical, sacramental, and ecclesial life if we are to respond to the postmodern age in which having fun is an ideological imperative of market forces.

Coming out of the European experience of World War II, Donald MacKinnon inspired a generation of modern theologians like Rowan Williams to turn to literary and lived tragedy as a way of addressing the gospel news in the light of the horrors of the century. Tragedy reflects on our contingency, our finitude, and our brokenness; tragedy testifies to the fallen world even if the finite world is not tragic as such. What tragedy does is throw light onto our sinful tendencies, that is, our disordered and misplaced desire in the negotiation of our contingent relations, both human and divine. Tragedy, as Williams tells us, highlights how "the roots of our difficulties lie at the roots of our very sense of selfhood, so that the disruptive narrative that reopens the path to primitive levels of trauma and fear is a necessary part of how we live in and with difficulty and how we tell ourselves the truth."[1]

Arguably the significance of MacKinnon's work was his ability to traverse theology and the arts, bringing insights usually reserved for aesthetics to bear directly upon theology with a view to contemporary issues. By way of repeating (with a difference)

---

1. Rowan Williams, *The Tragic Imagination* (Oxford: Oxford University Press, 2016), 104.

MacKinnon's founding gesture in the light of our contemporary concerns, this book develops recent philosophical, anthropological, and psychoanalytical studies of humor to develop a theology of comedy as a rebuff to market-driven enjoyment. In other words, I make the case that in our contemporary age, comedy, understood theologically, might be better placed to account for our sense of selfhood and open up the pathway to primitive levels of trauma. As Freud understood so well, in comedy we also speak truth to ourselves.

In positing comedy as a hermeneutical key to theological self-understanding, I go further than both MacKinnon and Williams in regard of their treatment of tragedy and God. If tragedy is a result of our contingent relations, God is not tragic as such any more than creation and its accompanying finitude are. By contrast, I do not merely wish to say that comedy is marked by our contingent relations but that comedy is essential to the trinitarian life of God: God is comic, not in the usual sense according to which comedy relies on contradiction, and Christ's dual nature is the contradiction par excellence. God is not an example of someone who meets the conditions of comedy; God *qua* Trinity is, theologically speaking, the very possibility of comedy because God not only speaks but he creates speaking beings, which is also to say subjects of desire.

The reference above to Freud was not incidental. Psychoanalysis may be an interpretive method predicated upon the tragic dimensions of the Oedipal desire, including the misrecognitions that arise in the capacity of speech, but it also has an increasing amount to say about comedy, speech, and desire in a way that lends itself to the crisis of enjoyment in the postmodern age. And while psychoanalysis has long been set, or set itself, in secular opposition to theology, its contemporary forms also deconstruct that very opposition in ways that invite a conversation around the issue of comedy, subjectivity, and God.

By way of opening up the debate with psychoanalysis, this work begins by taking to task the question of why comedy came to be either marginalized by the philosophical and theological tradition, or theorized within secular reason in a way that pitted it against theology. I undertake a *ressourcement* of the comic dimension found in the liturgical experience of the Middle Ages with a view to re-harnessing the creative potential of comedy for ecclesial understanding. Drawing on psychoanalysis, my aim is to develop a trinitarian and ecclesial understanding of comedy that responds directly to the demands placed upon the subject in this age of global-digital capitalism. If, theologically speaking, creation has the structure of the joke, then the church's task is maintaining that joke through its nonidentical repetition. Understood ecclesiologically, the comedy of God (i.e., the church) might yet outwit the logic of our market-driven enjoyment and its accompanying anxieties.

Introduction

The great Irish comedian and ardent atheist Dave Allen would often joke, "I'm an atheist, thank God!"[1] Allen may well have maintained a staunch set of objections to religion given the harshness of his Catholic schooling. However, it raises the theological question as to whether anyone can really be an atheist (or indeed whether Allen would have been a comedian) without God. Allen may well reject God, but he relies nonetheless on the very concept he critiques. Hence one could easily imagine the sentiment of his joke rendered thus: "I am an atheist despite God!"—a

1. Graham McCann, ed., *The Essential Dave Allen* (London: Hodder and Stoughton, 2005), 6.

negative version of its common Catholic counterpart, "I am Catholic despite the Church!" In each case, the act of transgression still leaves the idea of God or church curiously intact such that the very criticism serves to subtly legitimize that which it opposes.

It is a problem that besets much theological thinking on comedy. Taken philosophically, comedy is often viewed in terms of its functional ability to provide some relief or relative transgression against an otherwise normative polity. Comedy takes on a satirical edge, invoked to provide some temporary release against what, at heart, remains an ultimately serious matter and for which, in the final analysis, laughter must cease: comedy serves to both critique and legitimize a normative theology.

Alternatively, one finds comedy employed principally in terms of its literary or dramatic aesthetic with the fundamental theological sense to be found in its reconciliatory ending, which speaks something of the final eschatological ending promised by the Christian narrative. If the fall was said to have alienated humankind from God, then alienation will be undone in the beatific vision in which we receive God's direct self-communication, an immediacy of knowledge shared by the angelic spirits and souls of heaven. Little wonder Dante's *Commedia* ends on such a note. Yet the sense remains, we must suffer still the brutalities of this life while holding on nonetheless to that promise of a sense of relief to come.

Rarely is the attempt made to consider more concertedly how comedy might be far more intrinsic to philosophical, theological, ecclesial, or indeed trinitarian reflection.

This book follows from an altogether different reading of Allen's joke. What if being an atheist is not simply won at the expense of God, but rather, what if God's atheism is the condition of our atheism and indeed the condition of comedy? What if the conditions that make comedy possible speak analogously into the conditions that make God possible?

Contrary to popular reason (i.e., taken in terms of the dramatic genre), comedy is not about harmonious reconciliation. Comedy happens when things go wrong and especially when language goes awry.

THEOLOGY, COMEDY, POLITICS

In a joke, we commit to various beliefs. If a joke begins with the line "Where did Hitler keep his armies?," the belief committed to is the context of the question, that is, a question concerning military hardware or personnel, not a "mother-ese" (i.e., baby talk) pronunciation of Hitler's anatomical arms to which the response (also in "mother-ese") is "up his sleevies." If the condition of comedy is also the condition of belief, are the conditions of comedy the conditions by which God can believe in himself? In short, what if the sets of relations that allow comedy to manifest in the first place are consistent with trinitarian thought? And if that is the case, is the Trinity a place where God goes awry with comic affect?

This last question might seem rather odd, but much of the literature that accounts for the theological appropriation of comedy misses precisely this point. When theology expounds a theory of comedy, it does so largely within a set of metaphysical presuppositions. Comedy, for example, in the final call, is said either to be on the side of materialism and provide a corrective against theological hubris, or offer us an

INTRODUCTION

eschatological promise of the final resolution (over and against the sufferings of our material selves). But in such cases, the poles are set: realism versus idealism, or the positivism of laughter versus speculative metaphysics, in a way that renders comedy in the manner of a Kantian stricture on thought, an epistemological limit rather than an insight into the absolute or thought as such; comedy is merely a corrective on the side of the given and hence operates theologically as a form of positivism more often than not.

The thought that comedy might yield an insight into the trinitarian life of God and vice versa remains underdeveloped not only speculatively but in terms of ecclesiology as well. By this I don't mean to argue simply that humor should lighten the exercise of our church life (although it should). Rather, how might a concerted appreciation of the operative workings of a joke and comedy yield critical insight for ecclesial self-understanding?

There are any number of reasons such considerations should be deemed necessary. Five will suffice. First, as suggested, if comedy is fundamental to reasoning belief, it ought at the very least to be considered in a concerted theological and systematic way on *par* with reason.

Second, Aristotle's claim that man is the only animal that laughs may well be contrary to the evidence. Nonetheless, human laughter tells us something very specific about what it is to be human: to be human *is* to sit on the threshold of the antinomy between human and animal.[2] Chimps or indeed mice may well enjoy a tickle and laugh, but human laughter acts as a key site of this minimal difference. Laughter contaminates us with a sense of the nonhuman.[3]

Third, it follows from the above that comedy poses a direct question and challenge for theological anthropology. As the very term implies, "theological anthropology" is poised on the very line that both separates and unites the human to inhuman/divine. If the very contradiction does not yield a comic inflec-

---

2. Aristotle, *On the Parts of Animals*, trans. A. L. Peck (Cambridge, MA: Harvard University Press, 1961), 281; Robert Provine, *Laughter: A Scientific Investigation* (London: Viking, 2000), 75–98.
3. Anca Parvulescu, *Laughter: Notes on a Passion* (Cambridge, MA: MIT Press, 2010), 4.

tion in the writing of the great theologians, theological reflection should nonetheless take comedy into account as a key site of theological investigation.

Fourth, where modern, and in particular postmodern, theology has wrestled itself free of the strictures of classical metaphysics and its antipathy to comedy, it has increasingly leaned on narrative, dramatic (including comic pageantry), and aesthetic categories as part of its contemporary apologetics. In short, there is precedence for the aesthetic turn within modern theology, which resonates with its vernacular past to offer alternative perspectives on the place of comedy within theology.

Fifth, given the mood of Europe in the early part of the twentieth century and the dramatic reading of the Gospel narrative, which had to choose between the twin poles of tragedy and comedy, theology had little choice but to overwhelmingly opt for a tragic reading. This was often expressed theologically in terms of *kenosis:* in the incarnation, God empties himself without reserve, pouring himself into the contingencies of world history with all the uncertainties that implies. Yet in contrast to the twentieth century, and notwithstanding its own horrors, the twenty-first century seems to overwhelmingly opt for the comic and enjoyment in a way that marks it with its own particular set of anxieties and worries.[4] The "pomo" of postmodernity once promised a panoply of pleasures to be gained from our global embrace of difference. Yet this has quickly mutated into "fomo": fear of missing out. The imperative to enjoy has become a mission for mirth, a mandate of the capitalist market and its subjects (fueled by the debt economy) to the point that even considering a funeral a somber occasion is somehow looked down upon as running against the fundament *joie de vivre.* What dignity might be preserved in the event of a tragic accident is now quickly expunged as the site is transformed by passers-by into a dramatic backdrop for a selfie—a moment of narcissistic indulgence. All this is unfold-

---

4. Ryan Dwyer, "Smartphone Use Undermines Enjoyment of Face-to-Face Social Interactions," *Journal of Experimental Social Psychology* 78 (2018): 233–39, https://tinyurl.com/y9y2nv2t.

ing as levels of anxiety within Western populations grow.

Yet the twentieth century was also fertile ground for reflection on comedy and indeed comic reflection. The absurdist challenge to the dramatic genre (e.g., Samuel Beckett) was accompanied by increasing contributions from psychology, sociology, and philosophy to highlight further the role of desire, power, and cognition in comedy; the twenty-first century has only seen a further discrete flourishing of these branches into the fields of linguistics, evolutionary biology, and postmodern critical theory (including aspects of race, gender, and semiotics). In short, comedy cannot be thought simply in the dramatic genre but is open to multiple approaches, which all contribute to our developing appreciation of the phenomenon.

The theological argument of this book is simple: comedy thrives on what fails. Yet that very moment also turns out to be expressed as a joy. This is not an academic way of saying, "God moves in mysterious ways," as if in the face of life's tragedies God has nonetheless secretly rationalized a wider plan, the final revelation of which will somehow make up for the loss. Rather, God's failure is *also* his success, and as I argue, this is intrinsic to trinitarian thought in the way it is to comedy. Or to push the argument further, trinitarian structures (as opposed to classical metaphysics) serve as the condition of comedy, our belief in God, and crucially, our ecclesial self-understanding. Properly understood, Christianity started with a joke, and our task *qua* church is to sustain that joke in a manner that literally outwits our current modes of enjoyment and their problematization within the late-capitalist market economy.

In writing a book on comedy and theology, one is immediately faced with the question of whether one is attempting to write a serious book on comedy or a comic book on something serious. In the spirit of comedy, this book chooses neither side but finds its enjoyment precisely in the ability to hold these two frames together. If there is a joke in the book, it resides in the argument itself.

This book is divided into four chapters. The first

chapter ostensibly provides a broad, historical overview of comedy in terms of its relative status within philosophy and theology. The chapter is framed in terms of a central question: Why was comedy ignored or rejected as a site of significant philosophical and theological reflection? The chapter is structured around a trinity of occlusions: the first philosophical, the second historiographical, and the third theological. All three cumulatively contribute to what I call a collective *comicide* (i.e., the killing of comedy). By outlining these occlusions, I make the case for a comic revival within theology.

Chapter 2 takes as its critical point of departure the claim that the idea of comedy is linked primarily with the social. In contrast, this chapter explores the metaphysical assumptions that underpin and subsequently shape what we say about comedy and its function. To this end I explore the modern critique of metaphysics, working in sequence through Kant, Hegel, and Kierkegaard to the postmodern turn. Comedy, I argue, is too often invoked theologically in a way that owes more to the logic of Kant's metaphysics than it does trinitarian thought. Hegel's criticism of Kant elevates the place of comedy and sets the ground for Kierkegaard's theological reading of comedy in a way that opens the door to a properly trinitarian approach.

Chapter 3 explores and develops the work of the French psychoanalyst Jacques Lacan (1901–1981). Lacan manages to weave together Freud's insights into comedy with an attention to philosophy and theology. As I argue, Lacan's account amounts to a speculative re-description of trinitarian Christianity. Taken together, an altogether novel approach to both comedy and theology arises, situating comedy at the limits of what it is to be a human in a way that is fundamentally linked to parish (i.e., parody) practice.

The concluding fourth chapter explores the contemporary significance of comedy and enjoyment in the postmodern world. Building on Jacques Lacan and Karl Marx's observation that capitalism is structured as a joke, it develops an understanding of how comedy works, which is consonant with ecclesiological reflection and the practice of love. After all, does not Judaism owe something to Abraham's laughter, after which the patriarch Isaac was named? In short, the chapter develops a theoretical understanding of comedy and theology to inform ecclesiological reflection; it advances the case for a socially comic and critically informed role for the church in postmodernity, a counter-joke to the joke of capitalism.

The wager of this book is simple: if the church can appreciate itself in terms of the nature and structure of a joke, then laughter ceases to be the final standpoint of hope; it is the basis of a shared and non-rivalrous practice of love and the mode of self-understanding *qua* the other, one that is marked by a certain (speculative) moment of negativity expressed in trinitarian practice.

1

The Three Elisions of Comedy

The Slovenian philosopher Slavoj Žižek has drawn attention to a curious act of censorship on the part of the ex-Yugoslavian authorities following the release of the film *Sound of Music*. The song "Climb Every Mountain" was removed from the edit.[1] As Žižek explains, when Maria leaves the Von Trapp family to

---

1. Rebecca Mead, "The Marx Brother," *The New Yorker*, May 5, 2003, 38, https://tinyurl.com/26khl37.

return to the monastery and contend with her conflicted love for the baron and her vocation, she is given a surprising response from the mother superior. At the point one would expect her to chastise Maria and bid her to remain in the cloisters out of temptation's reach, the mother superior turns to sing "climb every mountain," in other words, make good on your desire. The Yugoslav authorities recognized in this reply the true subversive potential of Christianity. Rather than act as an oppressive and repressive ideology, Christianity contains a deeply subversive message: against an oppressive regime, you should not cede on your desire.[2]

In a similar fashion, we might enquire as to the censorship of comedy from the Western theological tradition, popularized in Umberto Eco's *The Name of the Rose*. The story is predicated upon the existence of Aristotle's lost treaty on comedy and a series of murders that disclose the church's attempt to hide the treaty. On this reading, comedy is antithetical to

---

2. Slavoj Žižek, "My Own Private Austria," *The Symptom* 10 (2016), https://tinyurl.com/y9ombwxv.

scholastic theology. Yet, what if the attempt to censor comedy was less a case of theological resistance and more a case of the secular construction of history, which saw the transgressive potential in religious comedy only too well and thus sought to write it out of religious history? After all, as Michael Screech has argued, given a copy of Erasmus's *In Praise of Folly*, one might be forgiven for thinking that the Reformation started with the laughter indicative of the comic insight into the contradiction implied in church abuses.[3]

This chapter charts three elisions, three attempts to cut comedy from the Western philosophical and theological tradition. The elisions are in turn philosophical, historical, and theological: three turns of the screw, each one contributing to a veritable comicide that impoverishes not only comedy but also what we might have to gain theologically from the insights this phenomenon has garnered both philosophically and historically.

---

3. Michael Screech, *Laughter at the Foot of the Cross* (Chicago: University of Chicago Press, 1997), 176–85.

I begin by exploring the place of comedy in Greek philosophy and its initial denigration, followed by its further condemnation in Christian thought. The second elision concerns an issue in historiography. Notwithstanding the Middle Ages, it might be argued that ever since the 1960s, Mikhail Bakhtin's recovery of the medieval Feast of Fools has in some part re-founded the comic impetus in theology.[4] One thinks for example of Harvey Cox's *Feast of Fools*, which puts the transgressive back into the festive with a view to the imaginative play with which theology should engage.[5] However, as I argue, the revival of interest in the feast is often cast as a critique of institutional Christianity in ways that belie the central liturgical place medieval theology gave to comedy. If, on the one hand, the so-called dark ages were considered to be without laughter, on the other hand, the historical recovery of comedy in the Middle Ages also falsely portrays comedy in a way that severs comedy

---

4. Mikhail Bakhtin, *Rabelais and His World* (Bloomington: Indiana University Press, 1968).
5. Harvey Cox, *Feast of Fools: A Theological Essay on Festivity and Fantasy* (New York: Harper & Row, 1969).

from ecclesial self-understanding and hence silences the laughter again.

More damaging perhaps, however, was the aesthetic turn in modern theology: against a background of twentieth-century horrors and the choice between comedy or tragedy, the latter seemed an obvious choice in ways that have come to shape much contemporary theology.

By way of charting these three elisions, I set the rationale for a more thorough recovery of comedy in the chapters to follow.

The Philosophical Elision

Philosophy has never been beyond comic reproach for its lofty abstractions and idealism. Take the case of Thales, the pre-Socratic mathematician and astronomer of whom the witty Thracian servant girl scoffed, for he was so eager to know of the things above that he could not see the well below his feet. As Socrates reminds us, "Anyone who gives his life to philosophy is open to such jest."[6] The philosophical setting of this joke and the very fact that Plato places this ridicule into the mouth of Socrates should already suggest the pedagogic significance attributed to humor within Greek philosophy: comedy is the materialist counterpart to radical idealism in philosophy. Indeed, philosophy has never been short of drunken revelers such as Alcibiades who, on entering Plato's *Symposium*, bestows his good wishes upon the crowed only to inform them that he is already pretty well bottled, a minor point that does not preclude his entry into the ensuing discussion.[7]

Plato and Aristotle on Comedy

When it comes to comedy, the chief interest of both Plato and Aristotle is the nature of pleasure. According to the two, comedy, like tragedy, elicits both pleasure and pain simultaneously. For example, when in Plato's *Philebus* Socrates explains to Protarchus his theory of "mixed feelings," he employs the humor

---

6. Plato, *Theaetetus* 174a, in *The Collected Dialogues of Plato*, ed. E. Hamilton and H. Cairns (Princeton: Princeton University Press, 1982), 879.
7. Plato, *Symposium* 212c–215a, in Hamilton and Cairns, eds., *Collected Dialogues of Plato*, 563–64.

that arises from comedy as an example of how the soul experiences a mixture of both.[8] Likewise, for Aristotle, comedy is

> an imitation of men worse than the average; worse, however, not as regards any and every sort of fault, but only as regards one particular kind, the Ridiculous, which is a species of the Ugly. The Ridiculous may be defined as a mistake or deformity not productive of pain or harm to others; the mask, for instance, that excites laughter, is something ugly and distorted without causing pain.[9]

Three points should be drawn from the above. First, both Plato and Aristotle provide the basis for what later theorists would characterize as the "superiority theory" of comedy. On this view, comedy arises from the position of the spectator looking down with ridicule upon a given subject (albeit without inflicting harm upon the subject). Second, and crucially in terms of the philosophical fate of comedy, both Plato and Aristotle deem comedy a lesser mode of

---

8. Plato, *Philebus* 48a, in Hamilton and Cairns, eds., *Collected Dialogues of Plato*, 1129.
9. Aristotle, *Poetics* 1449a, in *Complete Works of Aristotle* (Princeton: Princeton University Press, 1984), 2:2319.

knowing in the approach to ideal knowledge precisely because of its admixture of emotions. Third, both Plato and Aristotle nonetheless consider the category of error as contributing to a wider pedagogy. For example, Alcibiades's eulogy of Socrates in *The Symposium* takes the form of derisory parables, which are nonetheless aimed at truth.[10]

As Lydia Amin has highlighted, the derisive and educative place of comedy is epitomized by Socrates, whose ugly, distorted figure makes him a figure of derision even as he offers a philosophy that expounds the merits of laughter.[11] Socrates's speeches are said to resemble *Silenus-statuettes*, which served as a casket for sacred objects. On the surface they seem ridiculous, yet the content yields a rational argument at the service of both virtue and wisdom. And while "some [of Plato's words] are infused with a spirit of comedy so pervasive that they become burlesque (e.g., *Cratylus, Euthydemus*), all of Plato's works reflect actual

---

10. Plato, *Symposium* 215a–222c, in Hamilton and Cairns, eds., *Collected Dialogues of Plato*, 566.
11. Lydia B. Amir, "Philosophy's Attitude towards the Comic: A Reevaluation," *European Journal of Humour Research* 1, no. 1 (2013): 6-21.

THE THREE ELISIONS OF COMEDY

comic drama and use comic techniques."[12] Hence, as Brock has argued, Plato may well treat comic drama with suspicion and denigrate the arts more generally, but he nonetheless makes key use of comic motifs and techniques.[13]

When the aesthetic note was rung in service of philosophy, it was tragedy that answered the call. Tragedy was superior to comedy. Tragedy deals with subjects of greater intensity, graver and more complex issues.[14] In comedy we look down upon the characters who are presented as lesser subjects, who are inferior to the audience. The comic character is in contempt of the Delphic oracle: *know thyself.* So the real distinction between tragedy and comedy pertains to the pathos created: the tragic poets imitate a superior course of action in which the error upon which the plot turns creates a serious sense of pathos.

---

12. Amir, "Philosophy's Attitude towards the Comic," 10.
13. R. Brock, "Plato and Comedy," in *Owls to Athens: Essays on Classical Subjects Presented to Sir Kenneth Dover* (Oxford: Clarendon, 1990), 39.
14. Matthew Kieran, "Tragedy versus Comedy: On Why Comedy Is the Equal of Tragedy," *Ethical Perspectives* 20, no. 3 (2013): 427–50.

THEOLOGY, COMEDY, POLITICS

The seeds of comicide were germinated in the growing criticism of rhetoric. Aristotle points out:

> Life also includes relaxation, and one form of relaxation is playful conversation. Here, too, we feel that there is a certain standard of good taste in social behaviour, and a certain propriety in the sort of things we say and in our manner of saying them, and also in the sort of things we allow to be said to us; and it will also concern us whether those in whose company we speak or to whom we listen conform to the same rules of propriety. And it is clear that in these matters too it is possible either to exceed or to fall short of the mean.[15]

And,

> As for jests, since they may sometimes be useful in debates, the advice of Gorgias was good—to confound the opponents' earnest with jest and their jest with earnest. We have stated in the *Poetics* how many kinds of jests there are, some of them becoming a gentleman, others not. You should therefore choose the kind that suits you. Irony is more gentlemanly than buffoonery; for the first is employed on one's own account, the second on that of another.[16]

---

15. Aristotle, *Nicomachean Ethics*, trans. J. A. K. Thomson (Middlesex: Penguin, 1974), 134s36.
16. Aristotle, *Ars Rhetorica*, trans. W. D. Ross (Oxford: Clarendon, 1959), 3.18.7.

THE THREE ELISIONS OF COMEDY

As Amir highlights, writers like Cicero continued to find favor with the Stoic-peripatetic tradition of liberal jest;[17] *eutrapelia* (εὐτραπελία), or "wittiness," was a virtue to be exercised as a mean between the extremes of boorishness (ἀγροικία) and buffoonery (βωμολοχία). However, *eutrapelia* gradually gained a pejorative sense. On the one hand the Epicurean and the Stoic schools rejected irony on the basis that it involved a kind of rhetorical artifice, which was incommensurate with the pursuit of truth.[18] On the other hand, Cynics "hardened [Socratic] irony to sardonic laughter at the follies of man."[19] This distrust of comedy as a rhetorical device that undermined the pursuit of reasoned truth would eventually find its parallel in the modern denigration of rhetoric by the architect of modernity, Kant.

> Rhetoric, so far as this is taken to mean the art of persuasion, i.e., the art of deluding by means of a fair semblance (as *ars oratoria*), and not merely excellence of

---

17. Amir, "Philosophy's Attitude towards the Comic," 12.
18. Amir, "Philosophy's Attitude towards the Comic," 10.
19. D. R. Dudley, *A History of Cynicism: From Diogenes to the 6th Century A.D.* (Hildesheim: Georg Olms, 1967), 1.

25

speech (eloquence and style), is a dialectic, which borrows from poetry only so much as is necessary to win over men's minds to the side of the speaker before they have weighed the matter, and to rob their verdict of its freedom. Hence it can be recommended neither for the bar nor the pulpit.[20]

The negative sense of *eutrapelia* was consolidated with the subsequent rise of Christianity. In Ephesians, Saint Paul places *eutrapelia* among the vices to be avoided: "Nor should there be obscenity, foolish talk or coarse joking, which are out of place, but rather thanksgiving" (Eph 5:4). Wit was further condemned by the roll call of patristic authors (both East and West).[21] Clement of Alexandria, like Aristotle, might well have thought that man was the only animal that laughed, but he remains uneasy: laughter must be regulated, after all: "a horse neighs, yet he does not neigh at everything."[22]

---

20. Immanuel Kant, *Kant's Critique of Aesthetic Judgment* (Oxford: Clarendon, 1911), 192.
21. Ingvild Gilhus, *Laughing Gods, Weeping Virgins: Laughter in the History of Religion* (London: Routledge, 1997), 60–77.
22. Clement of Alexandria, *Paidagogos: Christ the Educator*, trans S. Wood, in *The Fathers of the Church*, vol. 23 (Washington, DC: Catholic University of America Press, 1954), 46.

As Gilhus points out, this unease was part of a general unease on the part of Stoic antiquity toward the body, which was and is overwhelmingly associated with the site of comedy; the body should be controlled just as reason should control the emotions. With the subsequent influence of Ambrose, Jerome, Basil, and John Chrysostom, not only is comedy condemned, but weeping over the wretchedness of this world is positively praised as a Christian virtue. Again, as Amir points out, "Christian Saints rarely laugh except in defiance of imminent martyrdom."[23]

Aquinas on Comedy

Not until around the thirteenth century was Aquinas (in response to Ambrose) able to re-codify the terms under which laughter was permissible. In Question 168 of the *Summa*, Aquinas deals with the question of whether there can be a virtue about games and the sin that arises in respect to the lack or excess of mirth. Drawing on Augustine, Aquinas revises the

---

23. Lydia B. Amir, *Humor and the Good Life in Modern Philosophy: Shaftesbury, Hamann, Kierkegaard* (Albany: SUNY Press, 2014), 200.

place Aristotle gave to *eutrapelia*.[24] For Aquinas, just as the body needs rest, so does the soul, and humor slackens the tension of the reason's study. However, fun should benefit the hour, and care should be taken not to insult but uplift the mind with care for the context. So, while an excess of mirth risks both mortal sin and venial sins, it also follows that a lack of mirth is less sinful than an excess, but a sin nonetheless to the extent it remains unguided by reason; it is against reason, for example, for anyone to be burdensome upon another by refraining from offering pleasure or hindering their enjoyment.

However, on this reading, the exercise of humor remains governed by reason. Hence, while the use of comedy may provide light relief, joking should not be incompatible with the gravity of the subject, that is, sacred doctrine. As Aquinas points out, while Ambrose does not altogether exclude fun from human speech, he does exclude it from sacred doctrine: "Although jokes are at times fitting and pleas-

---

24. Thomas Aquinas, *Summa theologiae*, trans. Fathers of the English Dominican Province (Online Edition: 2017), II-II.168.2.

ant, nevertheless they are incompatible with the ecclesiastical rule; since how can we have recourse to things which are not to be found in Holy Writ?"[25]

While Aquinas may have provided some light relief for comedy, the place of comedy remained policed nonetheless by the dominance of scholasticism, and it was subordinated to reason in ways that would stifle the legacy of vernacular laughter in the histories to come and reaffirm the classical tension between Democritus and Heraclitus presented by Seneca: "Heraclitus would shed tears whenever he went out in public—Democritus laughed. One saw the whole as a parade of miseries, the other of follies."[26] The philosophical distrust of the aesthetic modes, denigration of rhetoric, and Christian distrust of *eutrapelia* all contributed to the philosophical decline of comedy and would find resonance in the modern period with the work of the Protestant theologian and Christian

---

25. Aquinas, *Summa theologiae* II-II.168.2.
26. Seneca, *On Tranquillity of Mind* 15.2, in *The Daily Stoic: 366 Meditations on Wisdom, Perseverance, and the Art of Living: Featuring New Translations of Seneca, Epictetus, and Marcus Aurelius*, ed. Ryan Holiday and Stephen Hanselman (London: Penguin, 2016), 256.

realist Reinhold Niebuhr, for whom laughter's place was in the outer courts of religion.[27]

The Historical Elision

In many respects, the endurance of Umberto Eco's *The Name of the Rose,* predicated as it is on Christian antipathy toward comedy in the Middle Ages and the belief that comedy and laughter will undermine the church, has served to perpetuate that very myth. It is a thesis that finds wide popular support for example in Erich Segal's *Death of Comedy* in a way that affirms the tension between materialist comedy and philosophical idealism. In Segal's assessment, "The church preached *contemptus mundi*—the rejection of everything terrestrial, to concentrate on the next world."[28]

Of course, there were swathes of satire and comedy to be found in both the Latin and vernacular traditions of the late medieval period. Jacques Le Goff

---

27. Reinhold Niebuhr, "Humour and Faith," in *Holy Laughter*, ed. Conrad Hyers (New York: Seabury, 1969), 135.
28. Erich Segal, *The Death of Comedy* (Cambridge, MA: Harvard University Press, 2001), 257.

reminds us that University of Paris organized an annual conference in the thirteenth century on the subject of whether Jesus laughed,[29] while the ludic *Lauds* of Jacapone da Todi testify to the central place of comedy in the vernacular traditions.[30] Yet as Hokenson explains, "When referenced at all, Latin and vernacular medieval farce and fabliau, not to mention *sermons joyeux* and *soties* were long treated as popular or vulgar modes rather than distinct comic genres."[31]

Why, then, was there an elision of comedy from the Middle Ages in the contemporary scholarship?[32] The reasons may have less to do with the Middle Ages and more to do with modernity and the revival of comic theory in the modern period. For example, George McFadden dismisses centuries of Christian

---

29. Jacques Le Goff, "Laughter in the Middle Ages," in *A Cultural History of Humour from Antiquity to the Present Day*, ed. J. Bremmer and H. Roodenburg (Cambridge: Polity, 1997), 43.
30. Nicolino Applauso, "Curses and Laughter: The Ethics of Political Invective in the Comic Poetry of High and Late Medieval Italy" (PhD diss., University of Oregon, 2010), 39.
31. Jan Hokenson, *The Idea of Comedy: History, Theory, Critique* (Madison, NJ: Fairleigh Dickinson University Press, 2006), 145.
32. Hokenson, *Idea of Comedy*, 145.

comic art when in *Discovering the Comic* he states, "The comic theatre was revived during the Renaissance with astonishing fidelity to . . . Roman times."[33] And Louis Cazamian's *The Development of English Humour*, written in the 1930s, which allies comedy to national/racial types, is more openly disparaging. Humor, he states, "Hardly came into its own till the Renaissance; prior to that time the mental capacity which it requires was not very diffuse."[34] Medieval humor was too derisive or vulgar and precluded the more complex laughter of what Hokenson calls "enlightenment tolerance."[35]

At stake here was the rise of liberalism and the shifting attitudes to both comedy and religion in the modern period, that is, the rise of liberal concerns such as equality and fraternity in the context of social unrest.

---

33. George McFadden, *Discovering the Comic* (Princeton: Princeton University Press, 1982), 57.
34. L. Cazamian, *The Development of English Humour* (Durham, NC: Duke University Press, 1952), 4.
35. Hokenson, *Idea of Comedy*, 146.

THE THREE ELISIONS OF COMEDY

The architect of liberalism Thomas Hobbes (1588–1679) revived the Aristotelian superiority theory: comedy is found in the denigration of a butt, which, in turn, serves to strengthen the existing society. Hobbes gives emphatic expression to the idea when he says: "Sudden glory, is the passion which makes those grimaces called laughter; and is caused either by some sudden act of their own, that pleases them; or by the apprehension of some deformed thing in another, by comparison whereof they suddenly applaud themselves."[36]

The reply given by the third Earl of Shaftesbury (1671–1713) that "it is not fit that we should know by nature that we are all wolves"[37] gets to the heart of the issue: we are not simply self-seeking individuals who, left to their own devices, would descend into Rousseau's war of all war. Comedy, on Hobbes's

---

36. Thomas Hobbes, "Leviathan," in *The Philosophy of Laughter and Humor*, ed. John Morreall (New York: SUNY Press, 1987), 19.
37. Anthony Ashley Cooper Shaftesbury, Third Earl, *Characteristics of Men, Manners, Opinions, Times, with a Collection of Letters: Volume 1* (Basil: J. J. Tourneise, 1790), 78.

reading, provides the argument for the imposition of law.

The brilliance of Shaftesbury's work lies in his recovery of link between humor and the *sensus communi*: a common-sense humor to assist reasoning and foster mental flexibility, thereby serving as a social lubricant. The Earl's objective was to challenge the English love of cruel satire in favor of a more gentlemanly and urbane wit by placating enthusiasm: comedy is socially pleasurable communicativeness.[38]

Taken together, both Hobbes and Shaftesbury highlight the place of comedy in the emerging liberal state, exemplifying the way comedy was implemented in our assumptions concerning negative (Hobbes) or positive (Shaftesbury) construals of freedom. Despite their differences, both employ comedy to support the liberal agenda. Shaftesbury's account, for example, quickly translates into the desire for religious tolerance, with comedy guarding against idolatry to placate religious enthusiasm in the social sphere. If, for Hobbes, we might make fun of Chris-

---

38. Shaftesbury, *Characteristics of Men*, 47–130.

tians for the sake of the social, for Shaftesbury, Christian fun is at never to be had at the expense of the social.

On the basis of the above, we might posit the following: if the comic of the Middle Ages was elided, it was because religion presented a mode of challenge to the growing liberal consensus and value of egalitarianism in the modern period, as seen on the Hobbes-versus-Shaftesbury debate. Seen from this perspective, the logic runs something like this: religion was subversive, and therefore its subversive humor of the Middle Ages was to be denigrated and elided for sake of the social. To put the matter more boldly, rather than the church confining comedy in the Middle Ages, it was the rising tide of secular liberalism that confined the comedy of the church in ways that would neutralize its subversive potential.

Bakhtin and the Comic Occlusion of Theology

It is tempting to think of Mikhail Bakhtin's (1895–1975) recovery of the Feast of Fools as a welcome riposte to the historical elision of comedy.

Bakhtin's thought developed out of his study of the French monk and scholar François Rabelais (ca. 1483–1553), who was noted for his work on the grotesque and bawdy jokes. The religious Feast of Fools and the festive laughter of the Middle Ages celebrates for Bakhtin the social body, a folk community ever growing through the cycle of seasons. For Bakhtin, carnival or festive eruption should never be a mere holiday or self-serving festival; carnival preexists the power of priests and kings and invites festive liberation from social restraints.[39] Yet despite his recovery of feast for our cultural imagination, there remains an ideological fashioning to his work that skews it. Bakhtin's theory tells us far more about the modern prejudice against religion than it does the Christian Feast of Fools.

Where eighteenth- and nineteenth-century theories of laughter tended to denigrate as vulgar the corporeal and derogative humor of the Middle Ages—what Bakhtin called "grotesque realism"[40]—

---

39. Mikhail Bakhtin, *Rabelais and His World* (Bloomington: Indiana University Press, 1968), xviii.

THE THREE ELISIONS OF COMEDY

Bakhtin himself sought its recovery, championing laughter as a cultural and political force: "the lowering of all that is high, spiritual, ideal, abstract ... is a transfer to the material level, to the sphere of earth and body in their indissoluble unity."[41] This is the materialist bent of his work: comedy recalls us to appreciate our contingent existence in the face of lofty idealism. Carnival comedy becomes therefore "an expression of rebellion aimed at religious authorities and their institutions."[42]

The forms and rituals identified by Bakhtin are said to place laughter outside the life of the official church, and the tone of official feasts are described as "monolithically serious and without the element of laughter."[43] The carnival, by contrast, is the people's "second life";[44] laughter belonged to another world, a "folk culture,"[45] a disruption and challenge to the official feasts of the Middle Ages, which functioned to

---

40. Bakhtin, *Rabelais and His World*, 18.
41. Bakhtin, *Rabelais and His World*, 19–20.
42. Gilhus, *Laughing Gods, Weeping Virgins*, 104.
43. Bakhtin, *Rabelais and His World*, 9.
44. Bakhtin, *Rabelais and His World*, 8.
45. Bakhtin, *Rabelais and His World*, 5.

THEOLOGY, COMEDY, POLITICS

"sanction the existing pattern of things."[46] Laughter in the Middle Ages, Bakhtin informs us, "remained outside all official spheres of ideology and outside all official strict forms of social relations. Laughter was eliminated from religious cult, from feudal and state ceremonials, etiquette, and from all the genres of high speculation. An intolerant, one-sided tone of seriousness is characteristic of official medieval culture."[47] And because laughter occupied a liminal place outside of law, it is marked for Bakhtin by an "exceptional radicalism, freedom, and ruthlessness."[48]

Bakhtin's work implied a significant challenge to the age of reason in which theories of laughter and comedy tended to subdue the body and look down upon the vulgarity of the humor of the Middle Ages. However, much of the political thrust of Bakhtin's work is carried through his continual and crude dichotomizing of the traditions represented. Where laughter is now taken as "an individual reaction to

---

46. Bakhtin, *Rabelais and His World*, 9.
47. Bakhtin, *Rabelais and His World*, 73.
48. Bakhtin, *Rabelais and His World*, 71.

THE THREE ELISIONS OF COMEDY

some isolated event,"[49] it is, as Gilhus points out, an argument framed by a narrative mythology of the fall in which the golden age of pagan humor is lost in favor of Christian seriousness: "laughter becomes an expression of a salvific generative power."[50]

Indeed, as Hokenson points out, Bakhtin "mutes the theological traditions behind much of the carnival history he is citing."[51] For example, he readily "notes traces of Roman saturnalia in pagan humor as folk background, but neglects the doctrinal background of the Catholic Church, which sanctioned carnival." Bakhtin sweeps it all together as "folk humour."[52] Bakhtin repeats here widely held popularist theories of the festive origins of comedy that grew in the light of Frazer's *The Golden Bough* (1890–1915) and F. M. Cornford's influential study *The Origins of Attic Drama* (1914). If early Greek comic actors were depicted in phallic masks, one could easily sidestep

---

49. Bakhtin, *Rabelais and His World*, 11.
50. Gilhus, *Laughing Gods, Weeping Virgins*, 105.
51. Hokenson, *Idea of Comedy*, 117. See also Bakhtin, *Rabelais and His World*, 198–99.
52. Hokenson, *Idea of Comedy*, 117.

Christian comedy in favor of its historical roots in the subversive potential of the fertility rites; while the Christian feast is revived for its theological potential, the God of Christianity is quickly disposed of in favor of the god Saturnalia.

The Feast of Fools

The cumulative effect of Bakhtin's work and the general folklorist background informing comedy was not simply to mask the theological foundations of comedy; more specifically, it pitches comedy against the liturgy of the church. In short, the feast is elided from its liturgical context and placed under the rubric of drama. What, then, of the Feast of Fools and its place within the Western Christian tradition?

Christian biblical tradition generally acknowledges two types of fool: first, the fool depicted by the psalmist, for whom there is no God (Ps 14:1). The second type of fool is the one chosen by God for his or her "lack of worldly status" (1 Cor 1:27–30), those who are prepared to be fools *for* Christ (1 Cor 4:10). The Feast of Fools celebrates the latter. "The Feast of

Fools celebrated Christ's 'foolish' willingness to humble himself by taking human flesh and so to suffer the physical pain of circumcision and crucifixion."[53]

As Max Harris has argued, contrary to the usual picture of its exuberant and transgressive character, the Feast of Fools was an elaborate and orderly liturgy that celebrated the day of Christ's circumcision on the *kalend* (January 1).[54] The feast primarily allowed subdeacons to assume the leadership role in worship usually reserved for the cantor or bishop and was largely confined to the cathedrals of northern France.[55]

A number of isolated complaints regarding the feast surfaced around the turn of the thirteenth century and can be traced to Pope Innocent III.

> Priests and clerks may be seen wearing masks and monstrous visages at the hours of office. They dance in the choir dressed as women, panders or minstrels. They sing wanton songs. They eat black puddings at the horn [i.e., corner] of the altar while the celebrant

---

53. Max Harris, *Sacred Folly: A New History of the Feast of Fools* (Ithaca, NY: Cornell University Press, 2011), 68.
54. Harris, *Sacred Folly*, 6.
55. Max Harris, "Feast of Fools," in *Encyclopaedia of Humour Studies*, vol. 1, ed. Salvatore Attardo (Los Angeles: Sage, 2014), 237.

is saying mass. They play dice there. They cense with stinking smoke from the sole of old shoes. Finally, they drive about town and its theatres in shabby traps and carts; and rouse the laughter of their fellows and the bystanders in infamous performances, with indecent gestures and verses scurrilous and unchaste.[56]

However, as Harris points out, it would be wrong to assume this is an accurate account of events. Like many ecclesial condemnations, this is arguably an exaggerated and unreliable account of misbehaving. Historians have been further led astray by the reception of this letter in Chamber's influential study of the medieval stage.[57] In the collection of data regarding the feast the tendency was to privilege its ecclesial opposition and hence the disruptive power, thereby minimizing its contribution to seasonal liturgy while overlooking the historical development of the feast. Yet the narrative of disorder is incompatible with the lengthy financial and moral support for the feast.[58]

---

56. From a letter issued by the University of Paris, March 12, 1445, quoted by Harris, *Sacred Folly*, 1–2.
57. Harris, *Sacred Folly*, 3–5. Edmund Chambers, *The Medieval Stage* (Oxford: Oxford University Press, 1967).
58. Harris, "Feast of Fools," 238.

For Harris, it is better understood as a "joyous" liturgy for the feast of circumcision, "good humoured, and sometimes comic"[59] with aspects of inversion, even if it remained within a disciplined and solemn context. Its demise owes more to a falsely attributed over conflation with the general folk traditions, which made it the subject of rumors; it remained nonetheless chiefly liturgical.

Harris is keen to dissociate the Feast of Fools from other aspects of liturgical/theological laughter with a view to its roots in the liturgical feast of Christ's circumcision. However, highlighting the common aspects of liturgical laughter across its variety of forms also serves to strengthen a more general picture of the liturgical grounding for comedy and laughter. If the Feast of Fools was notably French, then tradition of *risus paschalis* finds its origins in Bavaria, while the York plays are English, providing a tapestry of comic sensibility situated liturgically across Europe.

---

59. Harris, "Feast of Fools," 238.

Risus Paschalis

The *risus paschalis* was the late-medieval Bavarian custom of including a joke in the homily of the Easter Mass following the penitence of the Lenten fast.[60] It might involve, for example, a humorous story that would cause the congregation to laugh but from which a moral could be drawn nonetheless. The earliest specific account of the *risus paschalis* comes in the form of a critical description in a letter dated 1518 from the Basel Reformer Johannes Oecolampadius to the Strasbourg Reformer Wolfgang Capito (c. 1478–1541). Oecolampadius was responding to criticism "that he has not salted his [Easter] sermons with jesting and jokes that were traditional."[61] Oecolampadius rejects the custom as "unwholesome," designed not to unfold the mysteries of the passion but merely provide some good cheer for the audi-

---

60. Michael O'Connell, "Mockery, Farce, and *Risus Paschalis* in the York Christ before Herod," in *Farce and Farcical Elements* (Amsterdam: Rodopi, 2002), 50–51. See also Maria Caterina Jacobelli, *Risus Paschalis: E il fondaento teologico del piacere sessuale*, 2nd ed. (Brescia: Queriniana, 1991).
61. O'Connell, "Mockery, Farce, and *Risus Paschalis*," 51.

ence.[62] However, as Connell points out, ironically Oecolampadius cannot criticize the custom without indulging in a joke of his own. Oecolampadius explains that should he be tempted to write a treatise on the *risus paschalis*, he would dedicate it to the religious reformer Wolfgang Capito, punning that it would be worthier of Vulcan (the God of fire) than Wolfgang, that is, it should be tossed into the flames.[63]

Bakhtin was not unaware of the tradition of the *risus paschalis*, yet like the Feast of Fools it remained a "faraway echo" of the "licentiousness of the Saturnalias,"[64] wrested from its liturgical place to be narratively framed in its origins by pagan fertility rites.

The York Mystery Plays

As their title suggests, the *York Corpus Christi Plays* highlight the liturgical and collective grounding of this cycle of forty-eight pageants presented on the

---

62. O'Connell, "Mockery, Farce, and *Risus Paschalis*," 51.
63. O'Connell, "Mockery, Farce, and *Risus Paschalis*," 52.
64. Bakhtin, *Rabelais and His World*, 13–14.

feast day of *Corpus Christi* and associated with the rise of York during the second half of the fourteenth century. In the York Mystery Plays, each mystery (craft guild) performs a scene in the biblical narrative with the intention to teach in the vernacular the historical basis of faith in ways that exploit vernacular leanings toward comedy.[65] As Michael O'Connell explains, in *Christ before Herod* we find the story of passion elaborated into "something strange and distinctive, a farcical comedy in which the figure of Jesus is forced to play silent straight-man to the attempts of Herod and his court to tease a response from him."[66] The silence that characterizes Jesus's response to Herod in Luke becomes a farcical occasion for Herod's "overblown rhetorical blusters" in ever more desperate attempts to cajole Christ into speaking.[67]

What both the York plays and the *risus paschalis*

---

65. R. Beadle and P. King, eds., *York Mystery Plays: A Selection in Modern Spelling* (Oxford: Oxford World's Classics, 1984), ix.
66. O'Connell, "Mockery, Farce, and *Risus Paschalis*," 45.
67. I am grateful to my conversations with Francis Stewart regarding this aspect of comedy. Francis Stewart, "*Risus Paschalis* or the End of History: Towards a Comic Hermeneutic for Liturgy" (BA thesis, Durham University, 2016).

maintain is the centrality of the Easter laugh. Peter Abelard (1079–1142) provides the first Latin reference to the "laughter of Easter Grace [*risum paschalis gratiae*],"[68] and as O'Connell explains, his hymns for the offices of Good Friday and Holy Saturday help us see something of how laughter became associated with the Passion; each of his hymns for the two days conclude with the stanza: "Grant us, Lord, so to suffer with you that we may become sharers in your glory, to spend these three days in grief that you may allow us the laughter of Easter grace."[69]

Situating both the York plays and the *risus paschalis* as instances of religious farce alongside the Feast of Fools allows us to make a more concerted claim regarding the liturgical and theological context of laughter and its critical role in theological self-understanding.[70] Indeed, it may be argued that it was the farcical element of the pageant that vindicated the practice.[71] As O'Connell puts it, Herod may well

---

68. Harris, *Sacred Folly*, 36n14.
69. Quoted in O'Connell, "Mockery, Farce, and *Risus Paschalis*," 50.
70. O'Connell, "Mockery, Farce, and *Risus Paschalis*," 49–50.
71. O'Connell, "Mockery, Farce, and *Risus Paschalis*," 55.

expect Christ to play to role of the jester and entertain his court, yet the laughter elicited from the contradiction between Herod's power and his impotency in the face of Christ's powerful silence speaks to all those occasions of absurd preaching, while promising nonetheless the "triumph and laughter in the larger play."[72]

To summarize this section on the historical elision of comedy, one can say that it was part of a wholesale occlusion of the liturgical roots of Christianity at a time when the social concerns of the modernity brought into question the place of Christianity within secular society. This goes as much for Bakhtin too. It might have been prudent under Stalin's communist Russia to disassociate the subversive element in the Feast of Fools from Christianity at the very point he tries to highlight the subversiveness of this rite, yet in doing so he privileged its ecclesial opposition. In the same way that the association of the English Morris dancing with paganism owes more to the Reformers' critique of Catholicism than it did the

---

72. O'Connell, "Mockery, Farce, and *Risus Paschalis*," 56.

THE THREE ELISIONS OF COMEDY

beliefs or practices of the Morris dancers, Bakhtin readily attributes pagan sources to Christian comedy and then hurls the sources back against the theological institutions themselves. Indeed, the very argument of *Rabelais*—Rabelais's literature is the medium by which the folk customs identified with the Feast of Fools resurfaced and informed the critical consciousness of the Renaissance and its literature[73]—implies that comic festivity only survives when it disavows the institutional frameworks it relied upon and takes the form of literature. In doing so, Bakhtin shifts the emphasis from the active participants of carnival to mere spectator.[74] However, as Joseph Ratzinger put it in his Easter meditations, "Is there not something beautiful and appropriate about laughter becoming a liturgical symbol?"[75] One may concur with Hokenson that "it may have been simply prudent under the Soviets to omit theological questions, and Bakhtin is clearly chaffing against Stalin's authoritarian

---

73. Bakhtin, *Rabelais and His World*, 97.
74. Stewart, "*Risus Paschalis* or the End of History," 12.
75. Joseph Cardinal Ratzinger, *Images of Hope: Meditations on Major Feasts* (San Francisco: Ignatius, 2006), 50.

regime,"[76] but his work only serves to undermine the place of comedy with the church. Hence, against the usual populalist claim that Christianity suppressed laughter, one should entertain the counterclaim that it was the secular theorists of comedy that suppressed religious laugher: against the Christian confinement of the comic, one could make the case for the comic confinement of Christianity.

The Theological Elision

Our third elision is theological and two-pronged. On the one hand, we have a generation of theologians who, in the wake of the horrors of the twentieth century, positively embraced the aesthetic paradigm of tragedy as the proper register of theology. No theologian in this regard was more influential in the Anglican world than Donald MacKinnon (1913–1994). On the other hand, we have a group of theologians like Harvey Cox (b. 1929), who adopts comedy as a transgressive impulse. However, as I argue in regard of

---

76. Hokenson, *Idea of Comedy*, 117.

the latter, the theological appropriation of comedy is such that the resultant theology bears more similarities with the tenor of tragedy than it does comedy. In this way, the domination of tragedy is made complete. At the very least this should suggest, by way of a prelude to the following chapter, that if we are to recover the significance of comedy for theology, we need a more refined understanding of comedy. For now, let us explore in more detail MacKinnon's theology of tragedy.

Donald MacKinnon: Theology and Tragedy

MacKinnon's work is particularity significant, not just for the influence he exercised over theology in the late twentieth and early twenty-first centuries (one thinks for example of Rowan Williams, Nicholas Lash, Brian Hebblethwaite, Fergus Kerr, and David Fergusson) but because he develops a trinitarian theology specifically characterized by the tragic form.[77]

---

77. Andrew Bowyer, "To Perceive Tragedy without the Loss of Hope: Donald MacKinnon's Moral Realism," (PhD diss., University of Edinburgh, 2015), 4; See also the contributors to Kenneth Surin, ed., *Christ, Ethics and*

THEOLOGY, COMEDY, POLITICS

For MacKinnon, theology remained impoverished if theologians were unable or unwilling to draw on the wealth of human experience and culture. Sophocles, Shakespeare, Dostoyevsky, George Eliot, and Joseph Conrad all serve as sites of divine revelation.[78] As MacKinnon put it, "Did not Shakespeare *reveal* something new in his achievement of *Hamlet?*"[79]

Like his notable friend George Steiner, MacKinnon thought that the extermination of six million Jews during World War II was a staggering atrocity, and any theology that refused to contend with this fact could not appear as anything else but shallow.[80] As MacKinnon says, the events of Germany between 1933 and 1945 "rob any serious theologian of the remotest excuse for ignoring the tragic element in Christianity."[81] By contrast, Steiner took the view

Tragedy: Essays in Honour of Donald MacKinnon (Cambridge: Cambridge University Press, 1989), ix.

78. Donald MacKinnon, *Borderlands of Theology and Other Essays* (London: Lutterworth, 1968), 21.
79. MacKinnon, *Borderlands of Theology and Other Essays*, 50.
80. Timothy Connor, *The Kenotic Trajectory of the Church in Donald MacKinnon's Theology* (London: Bloomsbury, 2011), 7n22.
81. Donald MacKinnon, *The Problem of Metaphysics* (Cambridge: Cambridge University Press, 1974), 130.

that the aesthetic category of tragedy was alien to both Judeo-Christian theology and Marxism. All men may well be aware of tragedy (or as Raymond Williams, reflecting upon his father, would say in response to Steiner, "we come to tragedy by many roads"),[82] but tragedy as a form of drama is not universal.[83]

According to Steiner, tragedy fundamentally belongs to the Greek mind: "The Judaic spirit is vehement in its conviction that the order of the universe and of man's estate is accessible to reason. The ways of the Lord are neither wanton nor absurd."[84] Likewise, "Christianity is an anti-tragic vision of the world. This is as true today as it was when Dante entitled his poem a *commedia*. . . . Christianity offers to man . . . an assurance of final certitude and repose in God. It leads the soul towards justice and resurrection."[85] Likewise, "Marxism is characteristically Jewish in its

---

82. Raymond Williams, *Modern Tragedy* (London: Chatto and Windus, 1966), 1.
83. George Steiner, *The Death of Tragedy* (London: Faber and Faber, 1961), 3.
84. Steiner, *Death of Tragedy*, 4.
85. Steiner, *Death of Tragedy*, 331–32.

insistence on justice and reason, and Marx repudiated the entire concept of tragedy. 'Necessity,' he declared, 'is blind only insofar as it is not understood.'"[86] For Steiner, tragic drama arises out of the contrary assertion: "necessity is blind and man's encounter with it shall rob him of his eyes."[87]

As Peter Leithart points out, when Steiner made the argument that tragedy was antithetical to Judaism, Christianity, and Marxism, he made the distinction between tragedy and comedy a matter for both theology and politics.[88] In contrast to Steiner, MacKinnon made the case that Christianity does indeed speak directly into the genre of tragedy.

MacKinnon's theology of tragedy is built upon three planks: philosophy, Scripture, and ethics. First, understood philosophically, tragedy guards against the hubris of idealism. In the philosophical debates of the era between waning British idealism of the late nineteenth century and the analytic turn within phi-

---

86. Steiner, *Death of Tragedy*, 4.
87. Steiner, *Death of Tragedy*, 5.
88. Peter Leithart, *Deep Comedy: Trinity, Tragedy, and Hope in Western Literature* (Moscow, ID: Canon, 2006), 40.

losophy, tragedy offered a "third way." In contrast to the literary genre of magic realism associated with contemporary fiction, MacKinnon advocates "tragic realism," according to which tragedy is not only irreducibly ontological but in a way that recalls our finite constructions. As Khegan Delport puts it, in the light of MacKinnon's critique of Kantian strictures on metaphysics, "the reality of tragedy forces us to a decision: we either have to say that tragedy is a construction of the mind, and therefore trivial or revisable, or we have to acknowledge the particular dignity of tragedy, thereby acknowledging its transcendent dimension, that is, something that cannot be constructed or reduced to the strictures of apperception."[89] For MacKinnon, the encounter with tragedy amounts to an "ontological intrusion" that ensures that experience is "not simply a matter of wilful fantasy or even imaginative indulgence, but rather a response to what is there."[90]

Second, in terms of Scripture, MacKinnon argues

---

89. Khegan Delport, "The White Line: Rowan Williams on Time and Tragedy" (MTh thesis, Stellenbosch University, 2014).
90. MacKinnon, *Problem of Metaphysics*, 154.

that there is a basis for interpreting the Gospel story as a tragedy to the degree we can read the story of Christ in terms of God's *kenosis* (i.e., God's self-emptying). In the incarnation God empties himself into finite reality and is thus subject to the limitations of nature simply by virtue of the historical fashioning of events. For example, Christ's victory is won only at the expense of widespread death (slaughter of the innocents, the subsequent persecution of Jews, etc.). In other words, both tragedy and *kenosis* find their kinship inasmuch as both deal with limitations imposed (chosen or otherwise) by the contingency of nature or law. To be sure, MacKinnon is not so concerned with the classical issues surrounding *kenosis*, taking them up in a systematic fashion—dealing, for example, with the specifics of divine divestment of divine attributes.[91] Rather, God's kenotic activity in the incarnation, like tragedy, retains a dogged commitment to the difficulty of the task and reminds us

---

91. Kenneth Surin, "Some Aspects of the 'Grammar' of 'Incarnation' and 'Kenosis': Reflections Prompted by the Writings of Donald MacKinnon," in Surin, ed., *Christ, Ethics and Tragedy*, 105.

that if we are to speak of Trinity or incarnation, "we speak of a deed done in history."[92] God's coming to know the world through the self-limitation of the incarnation and death of Christ is therefore theologically paradigmatic of our own sense of self-limitation.

Third, and in anticipation of the postmodern ethics of alterity, MacKinnon makes the moral case that tragedy should inform ethics. In tragedy, we confront the fact that we can never predict the outcomes of our actions; we are riddled with self-deception and aggrandizing, and the attempt to move beyond tragedy is an attempt to unsettle the unfathomable mystery of God. As MacKinnon says, apologetic eagerness should not lead us to idealized solutions.[93] It is not that he does not discern elements of comedy within the Gospels, such as John's "masterly use of such devices as *double-entendre* and in particular a devastating irony,"[94] but that when we do, we encounter "tragic irony," a presence within the evangelist of

---

92. MacKinnon, *Borderlands of Theology*, 102.
93. MacKinnon, *The Problem of Metaphysics*, 124.
94. MacKinnon, *The Problem of Metaphysics*, 125.

a "deep tragic quality" that becomes "quite unmissable."[95] For MacKinnon, tragedy trumps comedy in a way that affirms the classical view that tragedy was closer to the truth to the extent it dealt with more profound matters than comedy.

If my contention is that the tenor of MacKinnon's theology is tragic, it is not that MacKinnon does not have a theology of resurrection. MacKinnon's point would be that a tragic reading of the Gospels recalls a degree of indeterminacy manifest as a certain experience of loss.[96] Christ's redeeming work may appear still unresolved, but this is a key sentiment to recall in those moments when we act in hope. Hence for MacKinnon, the lesson of tragedy is that "there is no solution to the problem of evil; it is a lesson which the Christian faith abundantly affirms."[97] Tragedy, on this reading, does not suggest that evil is an ontological determinate of the absolute but a contingent neces-

---

95. MacKinnon, *Problem of Metaphysics*, 125.
96. John C. McDowell, "Donald MacKinnon Speaking Honestly to Ecclesial Power," in *Kenotic Ecclesiology: Select Writings of Donald MacKinnon*, ed. Scott Kirkland and Ashley Moyse (Minneapolis: Fortress, 2016), 21.
97. MacKinnon, *Borderlands of Theology*, 104.

sity that arises out of the result of God's engagement in time; in tragedy we encounter the deep abysses of human circumstances.

However, is this not precisely the place ascribed to comedy? As Stanley Hauerwas points out, Christians differed from the ancients in their claim that the world was created (as opposed to eternal) and that "comedy is made possible by the sheer contingency of all that is."[98]

The Antinomies of Tragic Reasoning

By way of criticism, it is possible to have some fun, because a simple experiment renders clear the basic issue at stake. One can simply replace MacKinnon's use of "tragedy" with "comedy" and retain precisely the same outcome. Taking MacKinnon's first plank (tragedy guards against idealism), consider, for example, the appropriation of comedy by MacKinnon's theological and literary contemporary Nathan Scott Jr. In a passage that recalls Bakhtin's association of

---

98. Stanley Hauerwas, *The Work of Theology* (Grand Rapids: Eerdmans, 2015), 231–32.

comedy with the body, Scott argues that "the great sympathy which the Christian imagination may feel for the testimony of the comedian is in large part a consequence of the extent to which it is governed by the same gross materialism in which comedy itself is so deeply rooted. . . . The Christian belief in the Creation and the Incarnation makes for a kind of profound respect for nature and time and history which is not easily to be found elsewhere in the history of religions." Comedy is "against all the various forms of Idealism and Gnosticism, to emphasize the genuine reality of finite existence."[99] For Scott, comedy like tragedy offers a third way, guarding against the hubris of idealism while maintaining hope.

Taking MacKinnon's second plank (*kenosis* and tragedy), can it not be argued that one could just as easily describe the gospel story in terms of both the comic dramatic mode and God's kenotic activity? Peter Berger makes the identification of Christ, laughter, and *kenosis*: God's descent from infinite

---

99. Nathan Scott Jr., "The Bias of Comedy and the Narrow Escape into Faith," *The Christian Scholar* 44 (1961): 33.

majesty is of itself a kind of comic inversion, "the royal fool," and hence to be a fool for Christ is to "participate in and symbolise the *kenosis* of God."[100]

Taking MacKinnon's third plank (the ethics of tragedy) can it not also be argued that comedy informs ethics in the sense that it highlights our ability for self-deception and self-aggrandizement while resisting Stoic resignation to tragedy? Harvey Cox's *The Feast of Fools* (a Dionysian supplant to his Apollonian *The Secular City*) makes precisely this point.[101] Comedy may indeed appear an insensitive response to war, but the comic sensibility is able nonetheless to laugh at the warmongers: "It foresees their downfall even when their power seems secure."[102] Rather than tragedy, it is comedy that ignites hope and leads to more, not less, participation in the struggle for a just world.

---

100. Peter Berger, *Redeeming Laughter: The Comic Dimension of Human Experience* (New York: Walter de Gruyter, 1997), 189; Screech, *Laughter at the Foot of the Cross*, 175.
101. Cox, *Feast of Fools*, vii.
102. Cox, *Feast of Fools*, 154.

Against the claim that tragedy guards against totalization, the influential literary anthropologist René Girard has long made the argument that it is precisely the tragic form that totalizes.[103] Girard makes the case for a universal anthropological theory of violence and sacrifice based on his reading of the Greek tragic form, and to which the Gospels offer an exceptional alternative. According to Girard, violence can be traced back to the mimetic character of desire: we desire things because they are already desired by another; in the round of desire, the competition for an object or status inevitably leads to rivalry, and murderous violence is only averted through a scapegoat mechanism. A sacrificial victim must be found to focus collective envy. The death of the scapegoat placates the aggression and re-establishes the social bond. However, the mechanism of the scapegoat is characteristically obscured—the basis of all mythological thinking—because the scapegoat is a substitute

---

103. See David Bentley Hart, *The Beauty of the Infinite: The Aesthetics of Christian Truth* (Grand Rapids: Eerdmans, 2003), 386; René Girard, *Things Hidden Since the Foundation of the World* (London: Continuum, 2003).

victim, not chosen for any intrinsic quality as such. Only the Gospels are the exception to the extent that they are written from the perspective of the innocent victim, and hence they expose the mechanism for what it is: a tragic myth that sustains arbitrary violence.

In "A Comic Hypothesis" Girard provides a complementary thesis on mimesis: the perspective of comedy to present mimetic theory as the unifying sacrificial theory behind the classically given distinction between tragedy and comedy. As Girard says, "Comedy and tragedy . . . are very close to each other."[104] Girard highlights the mutual catharsis in both comedy and tragedy, which he connects with ritual expulsion and purification. "Laughter must get rid of something," Girard tells us.[105] When we laugh, "we are really laughing at something which could and, in a sense, which should happen to anyone who laughs, not excluding ourselves." This, Girard argues,

---

104. René Girard, "Perilous Balance: A Comic Hypothesis," *Comparative Literature* 87, no. 7 (1972): 821.
105. Girard, "Perilous Balance," 815.

"clearly shows the nature of the threat, unperceived yet present, which laughter is always warding off, the still unidentified object it has to expel."[106] In laughter, we turn ourselves into the scapegoat. If social cohesion depends upon expelling the violence that threatens the community by ritually casting it out and occluding the mechanism, then one can say that the sacrifice is turned outward (to allow for community cohesion). Comedy, by contrast, does not so much aid to shore up the subject at the expense of the other (although it can and does) but rather risks visiting the same affliction on the subject.

Nowhere is this more evident than the tickle, the proto-mimetic joke, a kind of pretend warfare. In the laughter elicited form of the tickle, one expels all air from the lungs (a *kenotic* activity) and is henceforth rendered helpless, succumbing to the very condition it seeks to ward off. The laughter elicited from a tickle relies on both the real threat to one's ability to control the environment while at the same time that threat

---

106. Girard, "Perilous Balance," 818.

being nil: the conditions for laughter are contradictory. This is the perilous balance.

That being the case, it might be argued that comedy, not tragedy, logically stands at the foundation of Christianity. Christ was not born out of tragic necessity; rather, Christianity arose at the point at which God was tickled by Jesus, tickled by himself in the way that only the kenotic laughter of trinitarian difference could account for. As Eckhart's analogy for the Trinity suggests, "the Father laughs and gives birth to the Son, the Son laughs back at the Father and gives birth to the Spirit, the whole trinity laughs and gives birth to us!"[107]

---

107. Meister Eckhart, "Laughter and God," Society of the Sacred Heart and Jesus, https://tinyurl.com/y77jstw7.

2

The Metaphysics of Comedy

As Hokenson's imperious study of the "idea" of comedy highlights, ever since Plato's treatment of the matter, each successive cultural wave has contributed to the fracturing of the idea. Comedy has been theoretically revised and recast to the point that one finds increasingly contradictory claims as to what comedy is.[1] Comedy, as an object of classical study (i.e., Greek), might have survived up to the eighteenth century, but the split induced with Romantic reflection was simply the first of many such splits. Psychoanalytic, cognitive, evolutionary, phenomenological, and postmodern approaches all vie for explanatory competence, advancing in ever-increasing critical responses to the perceived shortfalls of previous theories. As such, the theories demand increasingly complex understandings, and the terminology employed must embrace an eclectic standard that stretches the narrative and dramatic modes of understanding to incorporate further developments. Comedy might once have been a distinct genre, but it now traverses all sorts of theoretical boundaries and dramatic types.

Nonetheless, Hokenson makes a strong case for the dominance of the "social assumption" as the underpinning and unifying aspect: "the stage upon which comedy is set is not the soul, but always the world. . . . Historically tragedy, epic, lyric, and other genres could all be ethical, metaphysical, even theological,

---

1. Jan Hokenson, *The Idea of Comedy: History, Theory, Critique* (Madison, NJ: Fairleigh Dickinson University Press, 2006), 13.

THE METAPHYSICS OF COMEDY

but they were never primarily social."[2] Comedy is "universally explicated as a *social form*."[3] We can laugh with Aristotle at ugly deformity and thus assert our superior values *qua* law, or we can laugh with Chaplin, the social underdog, and applaud his critique of the established norms. Either way, the plane of comedy is social, and the distinction equates to the two major forms: satire and populist.

Her argument is significant, not because she is claiming that comedy can *only* take the social form, but that our assumptions about the social form of comedy stifle the subsequent understanding of the art form and its elucidation. As to why tragedy could be metaphysical, ethical, epistemological, or even theological, her suggestion is that the fault line lies in Aristotle's questionable dramatic division between the two forms.[4] After all, Socrates tries to make the case at the close of the *Symposium* that the same individual might be capable of writing both comedy and

---

2. Hokenson, *Idea of Comedy*, 17.
3. Hokenson, *Idea of Comedy*, 23.
4. Hokenson, *Idea of Comedy*, 260.

tragedy, that the tragic poet might be a comedian as well.[5]

The question of what the idea of comedy looks like when set on the metaphysical or theological plane is the subject of this chapter. Rather than undertake an initial study of the distinct way theologians or philosophers have imbued comedy with a metaphysical purpose, my approach is to examine first the philosophical/theological architects of modernity and their critique of metaphysics—Kant, Hegel, and Kierkegaard—to highlight how the shift in metaphysical speculation situates a given use of the idea of comedy. As I argue, when comedy allows itself to be situated by Kant's metaphysics, it acts as a stricture upon metaphysics and what we can know *qua* theology; Hegel's criticism of Kantian philosophy is significant because his theory draws comedy into a trinitarian account of the Absolute. However, it is Kierkegaard's work that is shown to stand properly in anticipation of a trinitarian and postmodern idea

---

5. Plato, *Symposium*, in *The Collected Dialogues of Plato*, ed. E. Hamilton and H. Cairns (Princeton: Princeton University Press, 1982), 574.

of comedy, which will be taken up in the following chapter.

Comedy and Metaphysics

The relation between the universal and the particular remains one of the cornerstones of metaphysical speculation: How do we get from the one to the many, or vice versa? The same is true for jokes. Taken at an abstract level, jokes often make fun of the interplay between a universal and a particular, or more precisely, a given universal and its particular exception. A woman walks into the doctor's and complains that she hurts all over; everywhere she touches, she has (universal) pain. The doctor says she has a broken finger (particular). A misplaced conception of universal pain is quickly shown to reside in a particular instance. Likewise, in the realm of what Freud identified as tendentious jokes, the comic protagonist can often be found to have occupied a place of particularity at the expense of the universal, that is, made the butt of a given social convention, or they are rallying against a social convention, undermining the standpoint of the universal by disclosing its particular standpoint. Comedy, like philosophy and theology, is engaged in challenging our unchallenged perceptual beliefs and very good at thinking about the relation between the universal and particular in surprising ways.

Kant

Kant's destruction and re-construction of the metaphysical tradition arguably provides the exemplary modern configuration of the universal and particular and remains instructive for the treatment of contemporary theology and its comic appropriation. Kant's rejection of dogmatic philosophy (the error of rationalism) was that it articulated metaphysical knowledge (i.e., knowledge of universals) through concepts alone, without recourse to our sensible intuitions. At the same time, Kant resisted the skepticism of Hume's empirical (particular) approach. Both approaches failed on Kant's reading because both work on the assumption that knowledge conforms to the objects of experience. By contrast, Kant proposes that objects conform to our knowledge. The mind is not simply a passive recipient of the senses; rather, the mind is active in determining and understanding those senses. A judgment we make regarding a causal relation does not arise because we perceive the relation as such but because our minds bring the category of causality to bear on the senses and facilitate the understanding. We are, for Kant, above all rational creatures who do not simply accept what is given by perception but actively understand the world in terms of the concepts and categories supplied by the cognitive matrices of thought.[6] These categories form a conceptual matrix that underpins all human subjectivity and by which we are able to cognize the world: a synchronic structure or grid that provides a uniformity of experience and is particular to us in our capacity as rational beings. We may well carry opposing views over any given topic, but key categories of cognition nonetheless allow for meaningful exchange.

Kant's transcendental deduction is an attempt to demonstrate that despite the split between the subject

---

6. Kant, *Critique of Pure Reason*, ed. and trans. Paul Guyer and Allen Wood (Cambridge: Cambridge University Press, 1998), 110.

and the object, there are key a priori concepts that can be deduced as correctly applying to objects of our experience. In other words, the experience of a given object must in some way conform to the categories of cognition; so, while we can know a given object through the determinations of experience (i.e., in its *phenomenal* sense), we cannot know that object in itself (i.e., in its *noumenal* sense). For example, space and time are not properties of objects as such, but all objects we experience are within the matrix of space and time; only within human sensibility does talk of space and time makes any sense at all. Space and time are a priori forms of intuition, transcendentally ideal and empirically real.

Transcendental philosophy attempts to make metaphysics possible again by limiting the claims of reason; we can know some things to be universally true of all possible objects of experience because it would be impossible to encounter objects that did not conform to the conditions determined by our cognitive faculties. Hence, metaphysics is transcendentally ideal and empirically real, a position that shapes Kant's epistemology: "knowledge is occupied not so much with objects as with the mode of our knowledge of objects in so far as this mode of knowledge is to be possible *a priori*."[7]

Kant undertakes a similar move in the realm of his moral thought. He sets out the a priori conditions for moral experience (practical reasoning) induced through the categorical imperative, the unconditional rational form for moral thought that all rational beings should follow: "Act only in accordance with that maxim through which you can at the same time will that it become a universal law."[8] For Kant, the imperative relies not on treating others as a means to an end but on the value placed on humanity as a whole, an imperative to determine law in the direction of the kingdom of ends for which God and our immortality must be maintained as a postulate of practical reasoning (i.e., empirically unprovable but

---

7. Kant, *Critique of Pure Reason*, 149.
8. Kant, *Groundwork for the Metaphysics of Morals*, ed. and trans. Allen W. Wood (New Haven: Yale University Press, 2002), 37.

the necessary condition) to account for moral obligation in the first place.

In short, Kant set out to establish the critical limits of our theoretical and moral reasoning. He developed a critical, rational philosophy guided by the autonomy of the rational subject that establishes our knowledge of the world, and he demonstrated how to act morally within that world with a view to human enlightenment and freedom.

Kant and Comedy

Kant's approach to jokes neatly aligns with his critical project. What interests Kant about jokes is that they directly pose the relationship between the rational and the empirical: jokes are caused by ideas, yet laughter pertains directly to sensory pleasure. In listening to a joke, Kant argues, an expectation is generated that is shown to be false in the punchline. The mental movement is not enjoyed as such by reason because reason only encounters a frustrated idea. However, the cognitive exercise of incongruity animates our internal organs, and the bodily motion produces a wholesome shock to the body: laughter is an affection arising from the sudden transformation of a strained expectation into nothing.[9] Kant's argument quickly turns on the hierarchy of affections. Wit, as Kant argues, belongs more specifically to the realm of gratification, a lower form of pleasure that pertains to our bodily sensations and is "without the least prejudice to the spiritual feeling or respect for moral ideas, which is not gratification at all but an esteem for self (for humanity in us)."[10] In other words, Kant makes comedy a theological problem to the extent it marks the line between spiritual and sensual gratification, reason and laughter, the mind and the body, thereby affirming the liminal place where comedy resides: comedy at the limits of bare reason alone. We can see the problem that arises at the intersection of Kantian metaphysics with comedy and theology in the work of John Hick (1922–2012) and religious pluralism. Hick employed Kant's distinction between

---

9. Kant, *Critique of Judgment*, trans. J. H. Bernard (London: Macmillan, 1892), 1.1.54, in *The Philosophy of Laughter and Humor*, ed. John Morreall, 45–50 (New York: SUNY Press, 1987), 47.
10. Kant, *Critique of Judgment*, 49.

knowing things *phenomenally* (as they appear to us), and *noumenally* (as they are in themselves). Religion (or as Hick comes to call it, the experience of the Real) is only ever encountered *phenomenally*, but it contains a *numinous* quality that all experiences share. The *numinous* is the genus of which all human forms are species and forms the basis for mutual appreciation and shared reason. Hick liked to illustrate the point with reference to the variously attributed comic story of the elephant and the three blind men.[11] In the tale, a king calls three blind men—representative of the various religious traditions—and asks them to feel and thereafter describe the elephant that has been set before them. However, in their blindness, each one feels only a partial aspect of the elephant: the first feels only the trunk; the second feels only the leg; the third feels only the tail. Employing the language of Kant, Hick posits this difference in terms of *phenomena* (the particular) and the *noumena* (the universal). The implication is that each religion is only a partial

---

11. John Hick, *God and the Universe of Faiths* (London: Collins, 1977), 140.

cultural manifestation of an undisclosed whole at the noumenal level. And the ideological point? If we can appreciate our shared religious impetus, then religious differences would cease to become the focus of contention.

However, note how the materialism of the joke: we only experience religion *phenomenally* yields an implicit idealism: God is *noumenal*. On the one hand the joke produces the necessary distance from God (in himself) to sustain the phenomenal belief; on the other hand, it closes off any real or possible understanding of God by relegating him conceptually to the infinite, transcendent beyond. In other words, when we adopt a Kantian framework, comedy is made to work within a horizon of immanence by closing off the finite self in relation to the infinite.[12]

Hick's pluralist analogy finds its "inclusivist" counterpart in a similar Catholic joke: "St. Peter is showing him around the various groups; the Jews, the Protestants, the Muslims, the Quakers. Then they

---

12. Alenka Zupančič, *The Odd One In: On Comedy* (London: MIT Press, 2008), 50.

come to large area surrounded by a high wall from behind which they could hear the sounds of voices and laughter: who is behind the wall asks the newly arrived to which St. Peter replies they are the Catholics, and they think they're the only ones here!"

On the one hand the joke ridicules the Catholic claim that *extra ecclesiam nulla salus*: there is no salvation outside the church. The joke interprets and critiques Catholic exclusivism (i.e., Catholic truth stands above all others) by way of including the representation of different religious traditions (i.e., the particular) within heaven. However, on the other hand, the joke leaves intact at the implicit level the very assumption of Catholic exclusivity to the extent it is still a Catholic heaven in which the others are included, just as the newcomer is still met by St. Peter. In other words, while it ridicules aspects of Catholic belief, it does not critique the exclusivism that sits at the heart of Catholicism per se; this is left unquestioned. Analysis of the joke highlights the instability of the inclusive approach: Catholic exclusivism maintains its position as the big other that determines the meaning of the field in way that undermines the inclusivism the joke aims to foster.

We can see from the above examples the way a basic metaphysical duality is tempered by currents of Kantian skepticism in the theological appropriation of comedy. This extends to those authors who explicitly appropriate the idea of comedy for theological reflection. One the one hand we have those who theologically appropriate comedy on the side of materialism. Nathan Scott, for example, claims that comedy spares us from having to be angles. On Scott's reading, the incarnation is the comic constituent of Christianity;[13] Jesus serves to point out the mistaken incongruity between our idealist aspirations and our earthly and grotesque realism (in a way that recalls Bakhtin). Jesus is, as Alenka Zupančič brilliantly puts it, "the God who slipped on a banana skin."[14] In Scott's thought, the incarnation affirms the materialist thesis: comedy is critical of metaphysical

---

13. Nathan Scott Jr., "The Bias of Comedy and the Narrow Escape into Faith," *The Christian Scholar* 44 (1961): 38.
14. Zupančič, *Odd One In*, 45.

speculation while assuming it nonetheless; comedy is employed as kind of Kantian stricture on the limits of what we can actually know of God.

Both Harvey Cox's *Feast of Fools* and Peter Berger's *Redeeming Laughter* adopt the idealist stance. Comedy is eschatological: comedy affords us a vision of how the world might be otherwise over and against secular normativity. For example, Cox associates religion and prayer directly with comic play in a way that invokes the Pauline "foolishness of God."[15] For Cox, comedy involves an exercise of imagination that invites an openness to what we have received and what is to come: "By praying, man shows that he is not a slave of the past, of the 'fact' or of fate."[16] Festive irruption (one notes again the influence of Bakhtin) thus reconnects us with our transcendent nature, breaking the bonds of rationality in play in ways that both recall the past and develop the future. Hence, Cox invites us to look for a relief in comedy beyond the

---

15. Harvey Cox, *Feast of Fools: A Theological Essay on Festivity and Fantasy* (New York: Harper & Row, 1969), 139.
16. Cox, *Feast of Fools*, 48.

merely material. Likewise, Berger casts comedy in the role of redemptive hope, a riposte for the disillusioned individual of rational modernity. For Berger, far from sparing us from being angels, comedy allows us to be "angels of vision" inviting "a signal of transcendence."[17]

However, consider Cox's reference to Hugo Rahner: "In play, earthly realities become, of a sudden, a transient moment . . . the mind is prepared . . . to be relieved of all the weights that bear it down, to be free, kingly, unfettered and divine."[18] The quote highlights the issue at stake: if the given conditions for comedy rely precisely upon the distinction drawn between rationality and fantasy, with comedy falling on the side of the latter, then ironically we come close to viewing life itself as phantasm, a mere illusion rather than something that directly alludes to its divine source.[19]

---

17. Peter Berger, *Redeeming Laughter: The Comic Dimension of Human Experience* (New York: Walter de Gruyter, 1997), 198.
18. Cox, *Feast of Fools*, 147. I owe this insight to Francis Stewart, "*Risus Paschalis* or the End of History: Towards a Comic Hermeneutic for Liturgy" (BA thesis, Durham University, 2016).
19. Stewart, "*Risus Paschalis* or the End of History," 2016.

In both cases, we have a theological appropriation of comedy that implicitly affirms a spurious dualism governing the appropriation. On the one hand, comedy is pitted against idealism and rationalism, sparing us from the demands of a transcendental God and the practice of virtue embodied in the angelic hierarchy; on the other hand, comedy is pitted against Weber's "iron cage" of rationality in a way that emphasizes the emotive and creative potential that a transcendent God might offer in the face of human capacity for destruction. In both cases comedy is transgressive of the given law; the former (Scott) "theological," the latter (Cox, Berger) "secular." In each case we have two variations of same fundamental structure; what unites the two is the split between a transcendent versus a material rendering; idealism and empiricism, grace and nature. In this way their theological appropriation of comedy owes more to the classical extrinicism of Kantian metaphysics than it does a more thoroughgoing and paradoxical understanding of life grounded in the Trinity.

Hegel

Hegel's criticisms of Kant are pertinent here as are Hegel's subsequent reflection on comedy. First, his concern (among many) was that Kant's approach restricted philosophy to the justification of objective validity by way of the application of the a priori forms of knowledge, that is, uncovering the foundational and permanent structures of the mind. Taken in this fashion, any given object of experience can only be understood by subordinating it to those forms. What this fails to consider is the dynamic of thinking and the constitutive role of our social worlds or epochs in developing our very capacity of cognition.

For Hegel the task of philosophy is not to set out what can and cannot be known, or in what capacity, but the articulation of the determinations of actuality. Hegel's speculative idealism, as opposed to Kant's abstract idealism, is therefore characterized by a concern for the relationship between self-consciousness and the forms of institutions that give rise to sociality. Hegel's idealism demands of philosophical thought that it not be undertaken as a purely analytical exercise in a vacuum from the constitutive communities that make thought possible in the first place.

Hegel took issue with Kant's moral thought on the grounds that it reduces God to a postulate of practical reason, thereby rendering God unknowable, which in turn renders freedom unknowable and therefore impossible. As the Hegel scholar Gillian Rose explains, for Hegel the rigid and extrinsic dichotomy in Kant's philosophy between the finite (i.e., nature, necessity) and the infinite (i.e., transcendence, freedom) precludes the comprehension of either: "By degrading empirical existence in order to emphasize that the infinite is utterly different, the infinite is itself debased."[20] In other words, the limits Kant places upon reason encourages thought to pursue an empty abstraction and leaves open a superstitious approach to what lies beyond. Deprived of all characterization, God is turned into "an idol, made of mere timber."[21] For example, is this not the basic problem that under-

---

20. Gillian Rose, *Hegel contra Sociology* (London: Athlone, 1995), 98.
21. Rose, *Hegel contra Sociology*, 98.

lies Berger and Cox's appropriation of comedy for theology? When comedy is rendered as a signal of transcendence, it remains precisely that, a mere intimation of something unknowable.

For Hegel, the Absolute can indeed be known. Hegel's Absolute is not the transcendent, big Other over and against the finite, as if the finite was something extrinsic to infinity (which, as Hegel pointed out, limits the concept of infinity by posing a finite limit upon it); nor is the Absolute something that existed prior to nature. Rather, there is only nature, out of which human consciousness and Spirit (*Geist*) develop. To speak of the Absolute therefore is to speak of the very site where antagonism, negation, and differentiation unfold with the realm of human action in the emergence of self-consciousness and for which the understanding always arrives too late.

As Žižek argues, Hegel is usually taken as a "essentialist historicist," positing the spiritual "essence" of an epoch as a universal principle that expresses itself in a specific way in each domain of social life.[22] However,

---

22. Slavoj Žižek, *The Parallax View* (Cambridge, MA: MIT Press, 2006), 32.

this is to overlook the significance of the dialectical method. Hegel's method begins with the interrogation of a given concept so that it is quickly shown to contain its very opposite. For example, if one generalizes the concept of "being," it quickly becomes so inclusive as to signify nothing in particular, an example of what Hegel calls the self-relating negativity of a concept.[23] However, taken together (being and nothing), the two positions yield an altogether novel third position (becoming) that maintains nonetheless the initial concept in its self-relating negativity. "Becoming" is a novel category because it introduces the concept of movement into being that arises out of the gap between being and nothing.

Hence the "ultimate insight" of dialectics is "neither the all-encompassing One" of Kant, nor the explosion of multitudes, but the split of the One into two such that the opposition between the One and all that is outside of it is reflected back into the very identity of the One.[24] To be clear, Hegel is resisting the stance

---

23. G. W. F. Hegel, *The Encyclopaedic Logic, Part I,* trans. T. F. Seraets, W. A. Suchting, and H. S. Harris (Indianapolis: Hackett, 1992), 35.

according to which one presupposes a dualist ontology and posits two opposing forces that are reconciled in a higher synthesis or unified whole. If Kant presupposes a split between knowledge of the world and the world in itself, Hegel's point is not to reconcile this split in a higher unity but to transpose that split into the One. In Hegel's thought, the gap that separates a subject from its substance is strictly correlative to the inherent non-identity of substance itself.[25] This is what Hegel calls the speculative relation: a relation of non-identity. For example, to read a grammatical proposition speculatively implies that "the identity which is affirmed between subject and predicate is seen equally to affirm a lack of identity between subject and predicate."[26] Or, as Žižek puts it, in the dialectical synthesis "*difference is posited as such, in the form of an inconsistent totality.*"[27] Reconciliation on this reading is not a "panlogicist sublation"

---

24. Slavoj Žižek, *For They Know Not What They Do: Enjoyment as a Political Factor*, 2nd ed. (London: Verso, 2002), xxvi.
25. Žižek, *For They Know Not What They Do*, 105.
26. Rose, *Hegel contra Sociology*, 49.
27. Kelsey Wood, *Žižek: A Reader's Guide* (Oxford: Wiley-Blackwell, 2012), 3.

of all reality in the concept but "a final consent to the fact that the Concept itself is not-all."[28]

Hegel and Comedy

Hegel had already linked the role of dialectical thinking to the comic as such. His insight that the nature of thinking is dialectical and as such understanding must fall into contradiction was of capital importance to his project.[29] In comic action, the contradiction between what is absolutely true and its realization in individuals is posed more profoundly than in other aesthetic forms.[30]

Hegel's *Phenomenology* unveils the series of contradictions that arise when one starts from the *a priori* separation of the subject from the conditions of its formation (e.g., positing the individual as prior to society as opposed to appreciating how society fashions us as individuals). The various categories Hegel

---

28. Žižek, *For They Know Not What They Do*, 6.
29. Hegel, *Encyclopaedic Logic*, 35.
30. Hegel, *Aesthetics: Lectures on Fine Art*, trans. by T. M. Knox, 2 vols. (Oxford: Clarendon, 1975), 1201.

develops, such as the "unhappy conscience" (i.e., otherworldly religious self-consciousness), sketch out the historical consequences of the split that arises when the autonomy of the subject is posited as separate from the substance (totality) of ethical life and thereby afflicts the substance of ethical life.[31] Likewise, Hegel's "animal spiritual kingdom" (and the comic inflection in the title should not be missed) highlights the false dilemma of the modern state—the rights of individuals and rights of the state. The two come into conflict when one acts in the name of one's subjective right on the basis that it is universal, when at stake is one's own self-interest. Comedy arises out of the contradiction, that is, when individual rights are the means to employ a supra-individual power such that objective freedom transmutes into the hapless subject.[32]

In this sense, as Gillian Rose argues, *Geist* ("Spirit") in the *Phenomenology* means first "the drama

---

31. R. Abbinett, *Truth and Social Science: From Hegel to Deconstruction* (London: Sage, 1998), 22.
32. Gillian Rose, *Mourning Becomes the Law: Philosophy and Representation* (Cambridge: Cambridge University Press, 1996), 73.

of misrecognition which ensures at every stage and transition of the work—a ceaseless comedy according to which our aims and outcomes constantly mismatch each other, and provoke yet another revised aim, action and discordant outcome."[33] Second, it implies that reason for Hegel is "comic, full of surprises, of unanticipated happenings, so that the comprehension is always provisional and preliminary."[34] On this reading, the *Phenomenology* amounts to a kind of divine comedy in that if non-truth and error are inherent to truth itself, "*the movement of the Absolute is a comedy.*"[35] It is a point neatly put by John Baldacchino: "If Spirit embodies the drama of misrecognition, comedy ensures that history remains contingent, and reason full of surprises. Comedy is the becoming of possibilities that allow us to engage in life's contingencies."[36]

---

33. Rose, *Mourning Becomes the Law*, 72.
34. Rose, *Mourning Becomes the Law*, 72.
35. Rose, *Mourning Becomes the Law*, 64.
36. John Baldacchino, *Art's Way Out: Exit Pedagogy and the Cultural Condition* (Rotterdam: Sense, 2012), 190.

THE METAPHYSICS OF COMEDY

To clarify the centrality of comedy for Hegel, it is helpful to recall, as Stephen Law does, that Hegel sees comedy playing a key role in the development of humankind contributing to the growth of Spirit and freedom. Poetry, of which comedy is a subset, like all art gives expression to the absolute to the extent it expresses the relation between the human (particular) and divine (universal); art is only truly art if it fulfills its supreme task

> when it has placed itself in the same sphere as religion and philosophy, and when it is simply one way of bringing to our minds and expressing the Divine, the deepest interests of mankind, and the most comprehensive truths of the spirit. . . . Art shares this vocation with religion and philosophy, but in a special way, namely by displaying even the highest [reality] sensuously, bringing it thereby nearer to the senses, to feeling, and to nature's mode of appearance.[37]

In the *Phenomenology* Hegel introduces comedy under the subheading "The Spiritual Work of Art." The section dialectically sets out the way art has represented the relation of the human to the divine, the

---

37. Hegel, *Aesthetics*, 7.

particular to the universal. In epic narrative, the narrator represents the gods through speech, with the narrative medium depicting the actions of the gods (universal) as the actions of men (the particular); by way of negation, in dramatic tragedy it is the actions of the actor—as opposed to speech—that re-presents the gods. Yet in both cases the relation between the two (universal/particular) is posed as a synthetic combination: the universal remains external to the individual.[38] In epic narrative, the gods' actions may well take the form of men's actions, but the universal remains unrestricted and withdrawn from the connection. In tragic drama the split is manifest in the actor's employment of a mask: the actor *qua* acting may well represent a god, but only in the capacity of an actor.[39]

In comedy we encounter the final spiritual work of art, the negation of the negation. In comedy, "the self-consciousness of the hero must step forth from his

---

38. Hegel, *Phenomenology of Spirit*, trans. A. V. Miller (Oxford: Oxford University Press, 1977), 441.
39. Hegel, *Phenomenology of Spirit*, 450.

mask."[40] In comedy, "the actual self of the actor coincides with what he impersonates."[41] Hegel's account of comedy as the final spiritual work sits in the *Phenomenology* just prior to revealed religion, that is, Christianity, making comedy the ante-chamber to revealed religion.

Kenotic Comedy

The dialectical progression follows the kenotic trajectory of Hegel's thought. Recall Hegel's description of comedy *qua* representation: comedy marks the end of aesthetic representation (and thus art in general) in the sense that in comedy the actual self of the actor coincides with what he impersonates. In the dialectical passage of the cross (Hegel's speculative description of Christianity) the death of God is not understood simply as the natural death of the Son, as if God's essence had already departed (the Docetic heresy) but the death of the abstract concept of God (God in his indeterminacy). God initially divests

---

40. Hegel, *Phenomenology of Spirit*, 450.
41. Hegel, *Phenomenology of Spirit*, 452.

himself of abstract substance by contracting into man; in Jesus, God coincides with what he impersonates. God is finally self-emptied on the cross (the example of love) such that "what dies on the cross is indeed God himself, not just his 'finite container' but the God of the beyond."[42] Following this double self-divestment, the single individual re-establishes the relation to the Absolute *qua* the community (Spirit) of believers (the synthesis of the individual and universal) and takes on the contingency of belief as the new site of universal struggle. As Žižek says, Spirit refers directly to the corporal body of the faithful who stand precisely as "[the] Holy Spirit of their community."[43]

Notwithstanding Hegel's comic outlook, this passage should be taken with all the negativity with which Hegel imbues his dialectical logic: the logic of the Absolute is the dark night of the soul, a kind of subjective destitution on the part of the Divine, encapsulated in the cry of dereliction: "God, why

---

42. Žižek, "Dialectical Clarity versus the Misty Conceit of Paradox," in *The Monstrosity of Christ: Paradox or Dialectic?*, ed. S. Žižek, J. Milbank, and Creston Davis (Cambridge, MA: MIT Press, 2009), 257.
43. Žižek, "Dialectical Clarity," 282–83.

have you forsaken me?," which stands for the plaintive cry of human subjectivity.

Hegel's kenotic reading of the Gospel story can be neatly summed up in Groucho Marx's comment to the Judge in *Duck Soup*: "Chicolini here *may* talk *like an idiot*, and *look like an idiot*, but don't let that fool you: *he* really is an *idiot*."[44] The joke relies on the (Kantian) split we introduce between the way a person can appear and what they are really like yet challenges the commitment, inviting us to view the subject without a transcendental support, that is, coinciding with what he impersonates. One could easily imagine its Christian counterpart: Jesus may look like a human and act like a human, but don't be fooled, he really is a human. Christ is not a tragic figure whose self-determinacy to die is balanced by God's determinacy of Christ's death; rather, Christ is comic: God's outpouring without reserve into human form, derelict on the cross. In classical literature, the gods occupied the realm of tragedy, which was represented

---

44. Leo McCarey (dir), *The Marx Brothers: Duck Soup* (Paramount Pictures, 1933).

by the actors; in comedy, God occupies directly the place of man to be finally embodied as Spirit *qua* the community of Christians.

Kierkegaard

Kierkegaard appreciated only too well the place of joy in suffering and contradiction; he exploited fully the double paradox of the incarnation in time. Inasmuch as one can claim to have an innate connection to the universal (for example, through the archetypes of the mind), that person maintains only the single paradox of a particular person who is able to relate directly to the universal. However, Christianity introduces a further twist of the paradox: the Christian relates not simply to God *qua* universal consciousness but to the universal who is *in* time, that is, the incarnation. For Kierkegaard, the depth of Christian paradox and incongruity makes Christ the "prototypical event of divine humour"[45] whose event transforms all human expectations on their head, even as

---

45. Søren Kierkegaard, *Humor of Kierkegaard: An Anthology*, ed. Thomas C. Oden (Princeton: Princeton University Press, 2004), 35.

his theology plunges us more deeply into incarnational joy.

Kierkegaard, along with the third Earl of Shaftesbury and Johann Georg Hamann, is representative of the Romantic revival of Socratic irony, with Christ now cast as Socrates to explore the folly of the church. God works in ironic ways to advance his purpose; it is faith rather than knowledge that is the answer to our ignorance. Christ may have been mocked from the foot of the cross, as Michael Screech points out, but his mockers are out-mocked by his folly.[46] Interestingly, the revival of comedy in this manner reaffirms something of the classical tension presented by Seneca between the weeping Democritus and the laughing Heraclitus, with Hegel now (unfairly) cast as the laughless philosopher versus the mocking sophist Kierkegaard.

---

46. Michael Screech, *Laughter at the Foot of the Cross* (Chicago: University of Chicago Press, 1998), 52.

Infinite Resignation or Infinite Reconciliation

Kierkegaard's contribution to this debate, however, comes to the fore in the conceptual difference he introduces between the "knight of infinite resignation" and "the knight of infinite faith."[47] You might say that when comedy is placed on the side of Christ, revealing the hubris of our idealism (i.e., on the side of materialism), or when comedy is placed on the side of God (to reveal our earthly distance and a signal of how life might be otherwise), they both pertain to what Kierkegaard called "infinite resignation."

Crucially, it doesn't do to think of this as a pejorative term, rather it stands for the first of two movements of faith, or the "double movement of faith." To put the matter simply, if the first movement of faith is our ability to relate to God *qua* transcendence (e.g., natural religion), then comedy highlights this very distinction. However, in the second movement of faith, we relate to God *qua* time, that is, faith relates

---

47. Søren Kierkegaard, *Fear and Trembling*, ed. and trans. Howard Hong and Edna Hong (Princeton: Princeton University Press, 1983), 38–44.

THE METAPHYSICS OF COMEDY

to the paradox of God incarnate. In the first moment, our faith is established with reference to a given limitation, as exemplified by Kantian philosophy (and hence the comic function reminds us of our embodied nature); in the second movement, those very limitations are shown to be the positive moment itself: in the same way that Jesus is not a limited version of God, Jesus *is* God.

Kierkegaard (or rather his pseudonym Johannes de Silentio) provides a helpful analogy to refine this conceptual difference. He recounts the tale of a young man's love for a princess: "His love for that princess would became for him an expression of an eternal love, would assume a religious character, would be transfigured into love of the eternal being, which true enough denied the fulfilment [of that love] but nevertheless did reconcile him once more in the eternal consciousness of its validity."[48] In other words, the love the young man maintains for his princess is idealized to the point that she is raised over and above the contingent realm. The young man begins

---

48. Kierkegaard, *Fear and Trembling*, 43–44.

to relate to her in the abstract as a universal as opposed to an embodied being. Taken positively, as Kierkegaard implies above, the tale highlights the way a contingent being (the young man) can relate to an eternal consciousness *qua* love. Taken negatively, the young man must then become resigned to a love that cannot be consummated; it becomes impossible for his love to be translated from the idealist position into one of reality. The lover must become resigned at once to the very distinction between the eternal and the temporal with the danger that infinite resignation consigns love to infinite contempt.

This is not to say that resignation does not carry with it a kind of fortitude as exemplified by Abraham's resignation to Isaac's sacrifice. If the knight is a knight of infinite resignation, it is also because he does not give up his love. But one can be resigned in one of two ways. One can either give up the infinite for the finite and join the chorus of frogs in the swamp,[49] or one can give up the finite for the infinite (as demonstrated by Abraham's resigna-

---

49. Kierkegaard, *Fear and Trembling*, 42.

tion to sacrifice the finite [Isaac] for the universal [God]). Either way, the distinction remains: an individual who relates or not to an eternal consciousness outside of time. In each case, the resignation is always toward a loss (the finite for the infinite—comedy from the standpoint of idealism; or the infinite for the finite—comedy from the standpoint of materialism).

By contrast, the knight of faith relates paradoxically to the universal in time, that is, Christ. This is the second movement of faith, undertaken by virtue of the absurd. The knight of faith is not resigned to loss but, like Abraham and Job, receives everything back in a way that outstrips any initial demand. Again, it is not that the knight of infinite resignation does not experience joy but that he finds a simpler pleasure through the transformation of a given limitation. So, where the former knight can only think the finite and infinite as external to each other, the knight of faith can think the two as one. Hence, the knight of faith experiences the kind of joy in which the infinite shines through the very ordinariness of life. If the knight of infinite resignation renders love impossible, the knight of faith radicalizes that impossibility: love is possible by virtue of the impossible:

> Most people live completely absorbed in worldly joys and sorrows; they are benchwarmers who do not take part in the dance. The knights of infinity are ballet dancers and have elevation. They make the upward movement and come down again, and this, too, is not an unhappy diversion and is not unlovely to see. But every time they come down, they are unable to assume the posture immediately, they waver for a moment, and this wavering shows that they are aliens in the world. . . . But to be able to come down in such a way that instantaneously one seems to stand and to walk, to change the leap into life into walking, absolutely to express the sublime in the pedestrian—only that knight can do it, and this is the one and only marvel.[50]

The above passage is significant in that first, it underlines the positive significance of the knight of infinity, that is, that they can touch an eternal consciousness, even if their return is a little ungainly; second, the comic sensibility, or rather the experience of mirth, is not a conservative function (reminding us of our normative condition) but a function of excess, the too-muchness of God's love and joy.

---

50. Kierkegaard, *Fear and Trembling*, 41.

THE METAPHYSICS OF COMEDY

To clarify, we can put the discussion in the following way that recalls the Steiner/MacKinnon debate: metaphysics is tragedy, the first movement of faith such that when comedy exploits the contradiction between the single individual who is linked to an eternal consciousness, it is resolved either infinitely (i.e., they remain alien in the world) or finitely (i.e., resignation to the unattainability of the eternal consciousness). Either way, the comic moment cannot but be given over to the pathos of an out-of-reach longing; either way, the comic moment descends into tragedy precisely because it remains constrained by the basic duality as we saw in the work of Scott and Berger. What is not considered is the double movement that allows comedy to be situated in the very impossibility of holding those two frames apart.

Likewise, we can directly map Kierkegaard's distinction between the knight of infinite resignation and the knight of faith onto the distinction between tragedy and comedy. If the knight of infinite resignation remains at the level of tragedy, it is because the knight remains wedded to a basic metaphysical structure. By contrast, the knight of faith takes the pedestrian nature of life and lets it shine through *qua* excess, not simply as the sublime, as if we only experience God in those sublime, exceptional moments (Kierkegaard was wary of reducing God to the aesthetic category of the sublime).[51] Rather, the excess is the very thing that mediates the relation between the two (immanence/transcendence), the irreducible knot that prevents the reduction of either side to their own sphere. Comic hope, on this reading, is not a mere supplement forever out of reach; it is the recognition that neither the finite or the transcendent can be reduced to each other, in the same way Jesus can never be reduced to purely human or purely God.

Deconstructing Theological Humor

In recent years Peter Leithart has taken the debate in an altogether more postmodern philosophical direction. Leithart enlists the help of Jacques Derrida

---

51. See John Milbank, "The Sublime in Kierkegaard," in *Post-Secular Philosophy: Between Philosophy and Theology*, ed. P. Blond (London: Routledge, 1998), 131–56.

and the deconstruction of metaphysics to highlight the implicit link between trinitarian thought and comedy. In the classical/traditional scheme of metaphysics, which Heidegger identified with "ontotheology" (a term first employed by Kant),[52] God is translated as Being, the ground-giving unity, which univocally assures the meaningfulness and presence of our being. God is the big Other, the lock in the chain of causality such that were it to be undone, the whole sense of meaning would unravel. According to Leithart, it is precisely this scheme that is structurally given to generate a tragic sentiment. Hence, the postmodern deconstruction of metaphysics anticipates something of trinitarian thought, which, Leithart argues, is structurally given to the comic.

Leithart's point is not the crass claim that only a Christian can attain the comic sentiment; rather, our understanding of trinitarian thought can be read back into the genre of comedy in such a way as to radicalize our understanding of comedy. This in itself is a marked contribution to the field: rather than sim-

---

52. Kant, *Critique of Pure Reason*, 584.

ply adopting an existing theory of comedy for theology, Leithart establishes a theologically trinitarian approach. If comedies "end well," then it stands to reason that the Christian story is divine comedy, but the category of comedy both dramatically and theoretically does not always imply a happy resolution as such; everything rests on how we conceive the category of resolution and the difference that a trinitarian approach makes.

According to Leithart, Greek metaphysics is tragic in a way that fundamentally structures the outlook on the relation of humans to the creator. Nowhere is this clearer than when contrasted with Christian thought. Greek history maintains a tragic outlook expressed, on the one hand, in the degenerative myth that from the golden age of immortals (i.e., men made of gold) who dwelt on Olympus, we descended to the iron race of men (e.g., Hesiod). On the other hand, this degenerative story is cast within an overall cyclical pattern, the last age of degeneration being a prelude to the return (e.g., Virgil). In this case, however, the return to golden origins is simply that: a return to the origin as such.

In contrast, "The Christian account of history is eschatological not only in the sense that it comes to a definitive and everlasting end, but in the sense that the end is a glorified beginning, not merely a return to origins . . . God gives with interest."[53] In this sense, comedy *is* what makes Christianity distinct. Hence, if tragedies (as George Steiner might suggest) are stories that end badly, and comedies are stories that (notwithstanding any given peril given characters might face) end well, then in Christianity "the characters do not simply end as well as they begun, but progress beyond their beginning."[54] It is important to note here the way Leithart's trinitarian approach radicalizes the understanding of comedy economically: Christian comedy does not merely imply a reconciliation of a prior prelapsarian condi-

---

53. Peter Leithart, *Deep Comedy: Trinity, Tragedy, and Hope in Western Literature* (Moscow, ID: Canon, 2006), xi.
54. Leithart, *Deep Comedy*, xiv.

tion, but one that exceeds the very terms of reconciliation.

The problem, put simply, is the nature of the supplement: metaphysics structurally assumes a given source (e.g., the One/Being) of which subsequent creation is a diminutive or lesser supplement. For example, in the given distinction between nature and culture, the latter is considered secondary to the purity of nature. This dynamic then serves as the basic antagonism that Leithart situates in terms of the Freudian parricidal relation: father versus son; nature versus culture; idealism versus realism.

What makes Christianity distinct is that the Christian God is a Triune God who stands in contrast to all other forms of monotheism and polytheism. Two key points follow from this. First, because Christ is *eternally begotten* of the father, that is, he is both the supplement to God and coterminous with God, the son is *not* in conflict with the father. In other words, Christianity is not grounded in parricidal fear.

Second, the economics of Christian trinitarian thought render possible an eschatological telling of the world in which its ends exceed its beginning. The significance here is not in the well-established link theologians make between comedy and eschatology as such. It follows logically that if the genre of comedy is taken from its dramatic form and defined (somewhat simplistically) as stories that end well, then Christianity is able to narrate history as the ultimate co(s)mic drama. One notes, for example, that Morreall, Berger, and Cox all take as a given that comedy is cast in the register of eschatology.[55] Rather, the significance lies in the claim that comedy as such is intrinsic to our account of trinitarian life. In short, we might frame his argument thus: if Christian eschatology is comic, it is because comedy is fundamental to the basic doctrine of God in the sense that what God gives exceeds somehow all intimation.[56]

Compared to the historical-theological appropriation of comedy, Leithart makes a considerable advance. He does not merely invoke comedy as a

---

55. John Morreall, *Comedy, Tragedy, and Religion* (Albany: SUNY Press, 1999), 147; Berger, *Redeeming Laughter*, 199; Cox, *Feast of Fools*, 162.
56. Leithart, *Deep Comedy*, xiii.

gentle reminder of our earthly finitude, or indeed of what treasures might lie beyond this mortal coil, but makes the movement of comedy central to the dynamic of both the immanent and economic Trinity *qua* excess: a movement defined in terms of a reconciliation that outstrips the initial beginning in a way that recalls de Lubac's articulation of the nature/grace paradox. It is paradoxically our nature to be graced in a way that exceeds our nature, yet in such a way such as to restore our nature to be precisely what it is destined for: the beatific vision.[57]

Much of Leithart's argument has to do with the way metaphysics, in setting out the relation of Creator to creation, creates a dyadic situation. As Freud (psychology) or René Girard (literary anthropology) have highlighted, dyadic relations tend toward conflict, envy, and the like. By contrast, the introduction of a third element can serve to alleviate conflict. In the same way, as Augustine puts it, if love of another begins in one's self-love, then love of neighbor

---

57. David Grumett, *De Lubac: A Guide for the Perplexed* (London: T&T Clark, 2007), 7–24.

remains precisely that, self-love. By contrast, when love of neighbor begins in God, love of neighbor is precisely love of neighbor.[58]

If there is a criticism to be made of Leithart, it is first that metaphysics remains a pejorative term. By contrast, Kierkegaard's phenomenology highlights how the pathos of comedy (infinite resignation) is itself already a movement of faith, even if it is merely the first. In this way he avoids the crude dichotomizing of bad metaphysics against good Trinity.

The second point to question is his commitment to the dramatic genre. Leithart takes seriously the idea that supplementation is the background problem to metaphysical speculation, which is properly answered by trinitarian thought. However, his discussion remains limited to the extent the discussion revolves around the dramatic genre. So while on the one hand he is able to transform the category of comedy *qua* theology (if comedies end well, Christian comedy ends endlessly well), his work does not consider a

---

58. Augustine, *The City of God*, trans. M. Dodds (New York: Modern Library, 1993), 387.

fuller, more nuanced appreciation of comic theory and form.

Third, he limits his discussion of the supplement to Derrida, when Jacques Lacan's concerted trinitarian approach to comedy would have served the argument far better. Indeed, nowhere has the nature of excess *qua* comedy been more theorized than in Lacan's work on comedy. And nowhere has an account of comedy been both more and less theological at the same time, in a way that makes the very presentation comic.

3

Comedy and Trinity

As I have argued in the previous chapter, there is a tendency philosophically and theologically to theorize comedy within a basic metaphysical duality, such that comedy is used to exploit one or the other side of the ideal/material divide. Yet as I have also argued, when comedy is set to work within such a duality, it often debases the basic comic sentiment by turning it into the pathos of resignation: comedy either reminds us that we are finite over and against the infinite, or it laughs down upon our human follies in the light of what is to come. Either way, we are consigned to a miserable finitude. In what follows, I want to explore the comic theory of Jacques Lacan, grounded as it is in the premise of Freudian psychology (i.e., the unconscious). Lacan's theory turns on the figure of the "third," the oblique object cause of desire. This "third object" is not only what allows for the transition between two given fields of referent, it also structures our economy of pleasure in a way that provides greater insight into the machinations of comedy. What makes Lacan of particular interest to this enquiry is the way he furnishes his account of comedy with the language of Catholic theology: comedy relies on a Trinity. Indeed, as I argue, his reworking of Freudian comic theory amounts to a "speculative re-description" of Christianity in the manner of Hegel,[1] only now from the perspective of psychol-

---

1. Peter Hodgson, ed., *Hegel: Theologian of the Spirit* (Minneapolis: Fortress, 1997), 7.

ogy; in doing so, Lacan highlights the ecclesial, sacramental, and trinitarian basis of comedy.

Lacan, God, and Comedy

God and comedy never seem far from Lacan's frame of reference. In the first instance, psychoanalysis is above all a talking cure, and "with a trifling change, *dire* [i.e., to speak] constitutes *Dieu* [God]." In other words, for Lacan, as long as we speak, the idea of God will persist as a hypothesis underpinning the practice.[2]

Speaking assumes a locus and guarantor of meaning in the exchange, a master signifier that organizes and gives structure to the field of meaning (i.e., the symbolic), be it the "supposed consistency" of our ego (what Lacan calls the "imaginary") or the presence of the other.[3] And philosophy from Aristotle to Kant has long equated the search for ultimate truth with the God hypothesis. But truth understood in psychoana-

---

2. Jacques Lacan, *Encore: On Feminine Sexuality, 1972–1973* (New York: Norton, 1999), 45.
3. Lorenzo Chiesa, *The Not-Two: Logic and God* (London: MIT Press, 2016), xiii.

lytic terms is always the truth of desire *qua* the unconscious, which, according to Lacan, is structured like a language. It is a point that affords Lacan a dig at classical theology: "God exists. The way in which he exists will not please everyone, especially not the theologians, who are, as I have been saying for a long time, far more capable than I am of doing without his existence. I, unfortunately, am not entirely in the same position, because I deal with the Other, the 'locus of truth' and the only place to which we can ascribe the term 'divine being.'"[4] In other words, if we are to rethink subjectivity in terms of language and the unconscious, we need also to rethink our understanding of God as a God manifest in the capacity of the other; that is, through relationships.

In the second instance, as Lacan says, "A joke is usually present, ambient in everything I recount."[5] Freud had already surmised that jokes speak the truth of desire and that their function *qua* speech tells us

---

4. Lacan, *Encore*, 45, 68.
5. Jacques Lacan, *Formations of the Unconscious, 1957–1958*, ed. Jacques-Alain Miller (Cambridge: Polity, 2017), 106.

something fundamental about human subjectivity. Lacan builds on (and breaks) with Freud by connecting speech, comedy, and God in a quite unique way to make a case that psychoanalysis speaks directly into the concerns of theology and theological practice.

Third, given the centrality of jokes for Lacan, it is tempting to read his theological references as rather tongue-in-cheek, but Jay Martin makes a salient point (in regard of Slavoj Žižek) that is applicable here. In situating the relation between Christianity and psychoanalysis, we might think of the "frayed knot" joke:

> A piece of string walks into a bar. The bartender says, "Sorry, we don't serve pieces of string in here." The piece of string walks out the door but returns a little later, having twisted himself in a knot and messed up his hair. Recognizing the piece of string, the bartender says, "aren't you that piece of string from before?" "No," says the piece of string, "I'm a frayed knot."

In other words, we are perhaps looking at the same point from two different perspectives, and hence the truly comic way to read Lacan is precisely in his ability to maintain and pass between those two frames.[6]

Before turning to Lacan's theory directly, it is helpful to recall Freud's seminal work on the subject.

Freud

Jokes and Their Relation to the Unconscious (1905), better translated as *Wit and Its Relation to the Unconscious*, remains a major contribution to the field of comic theory. Most often associated with the relief theory (comedy provides a moment of liberation from social norms), Freud's ideas are reflected in a number of comic theorists. Bakhtin's claim that "laughter liberates not only from external censorship but first of all from the great interior censor"[7] offers a variant of the relief theory, as does John Morreall's theory that comedy is a form of cognitive play that provides respite from the seriousness of thought. This recalls Aquinas's theory and anticipates its role in stress reduction and boosting the immune system.[8] The significance of

---

6. Jay Martin, "Žižek Has a Lot to Say about Christ, but Should the Church Listen?," *Church Life Journal*, January 10, 2018, https://tinyurl.com/y9pztkdf.
7. Mikhail Bakhtin, *Rabelais and His World* (Bloomington: Indiana University Press, 1968), 94.

Freud, however, lies in the way he articulates the comic sensibility from the standpoint of desire, making the link between comedy and the formations of our unconscious. In doing so, he is able to claim that jokes give momentary expression to unconscious desire in circumstances where it would be otherwise unacceptable.

Freud's work on jokes (1905) followed closely after his magisterial *Interpretation of Dreams*. It was, in part, a response to Wilhelm Fliess's (1858–1928) observation that dreams were full of jokes that convinced him of the need for a concerted examination of the phenomena. Freud's subsequent theory of jokes arguably serves to condense his entire theory of the unconscious to the extent that while dreams may be the royal road to the unconscious, jokes offer us a cheeky shortcut.

Freud had already identified in dreamwork the role of condensation and displacement.[9] In the former, an

---

8. John Morreall, "A New Theory of Comedy," in *The Philosophy of Laughter and Humor*, ed. John Morreall (New York: SUNY Press, 1987), 128–38.

image that arises in a dream can be become overdetermined, channeling any number of issues through a single image. By condensing anxieties into an image, the image acts as a kind of censor, speaking a truth even as it veils it. In displacement, the cathected energy is detached along a chain of inference such as a phobic object. Both notions (condensation/displacement) are governed for Freud by the economics of a subject's *libido*, which accounts for the way in which we both identify with a given thing (condensation) or resist identification (displacement). In his work on *Witz*, Freud made the link between the operations of jokes with the dreamwork. For example, puns employ condensation (i.e., abridging two meanings into a single word); jokes, by contrast, often rely on a chain of thoughts or inferences that mask the intended outcome.

For Freud then, a joke relies on the social norm and the restraint it places upon our desire (the reality principle); in the process, the subject must maintain

---

9. S. Freud, *The Interpretation of Dreams*, vol. 5 (London: Hogarth, 1960), 648.

or create a psychical inhibition with a view to social norms and for which an expenditure of psychical energy is required. Hence, as Freud explains, "When pleasure is obtained from a tendentious joke, it is therefore plausible to suppose that *this yield of pleasure corresponds to the psychical expenditure that is saved.*"[10] Jokes render most visible the operative laws of the unconscious, demonstrating the tensions that manifest between the pleasure principle and the reality principle, with the level of laughter elicited from a joke corresponding to the level of psychic energy saved through the discharge.

As Jerry Flieger summarizes, jokes, like the unconscious, veil in three ways. First, they must mask the punchline so as to generate surprise; second, they must lure the listener in, presenting a joke within the field of what initially constitutes a common understanding; third, they must mask the operative desire (e.g., a sexual or aggressive impulse) that underlies the very delivery of a joke.[11]

---

10. S. Freud, *Jokes and Their Relation to the Unconscious,* vol. 8 (London: Hogarth, 1960), 118. Italics in original.

THEOLOGY, COMEDY, POLITICS

Like Freud, Lacan took jokes and comedy as a privileged function in the formations of the unconscious. However, by linking the unconscious to language, he was able to give considerable scope in developing Freud's theory of comedy and what it tells us about the human subject *qua* the pleasure of comedy. Drawing on the linguist Roman Jacobson, Lacan was able to make the link between the linguistic function of metaphor and the function of condensation in the dreamwork, and likewise the linguistic function of metonym with displacement. In this way, he underlined the relation between subjectivity and language: the link between the function of the signifier in the unconscious and speech alike. Metaphors, inasmuch as they substitute one term for another, operate according to a form of repression; metonym, by linking one word to another, operates in the manner of the successive chain of desire: the motor of language.[12]

---

11. Jerry Flieger, *The Purloined Punch Line: Freud's Comic Theory and the Postmodern Text* (Baltimore: Johns Hopkins University Press, 1991), 93.
12. Flieger, *Purloined Punch Line*, 103. See also J. Lacan, *Écrits: The First*

Formations of the Unconscious

Lacan's theory of comedy works within a basic duality yet in a way that problematizes that duality to present a third object. Consider on a simple level the way the ritual transition between two fields (e.g., the Oedipal conflict) involves the loss of something (castration), which subsequently manifests negatively *qua* desire: we seek something to make up for the loss (the return), but it is of itself a mere signifier of the lack for which there was no original and hence no possible recovery thereof. Lacan calls this signifier the *objet petit a* or *object a*, the small object of desire that sets us desiring and shapes our relation to desiring as such.[13]

Lacan's *Seminar* on comedy poses the issue of subjectivity and comedy in the following way: as humans we have basic needs (e.g., food, warmth), but as soon as we express those needs, we enter the domain of language and pour those needs into the "signifying complex," after which needs become

Complete Edition in English, trans. B. Fink (New York: Norton, 2006), 799–800.

13. The "*a*" of "*object a*" refers to the French "*a*" of *autre*: "other."

demands (i.e., what separates a need from a demand is the function of language). A demand is excessive of need. By subjecting a raw need to signifiers, what manifests is not merely the translation of a raw need into language; rather, needs are "captured"[14] by language and the polysemous nature of a sign and remodeled to create desire: desire is a need with signifiers such that in any given demand, something more is manifest that corresponds to desire. Put another way, desire arises when demand introduces a need into the symbolic order.[15] This is why any demand, even a simple demand, can appear excessive.

Jokes arise from this central dynamic: "Witticisms unfold in the dimension of metaphor, that is, beyond signifiers, insofar as when you try to signify something with a signifier, you will always signify something else, whatever you do."[16] Any signifier articulated in a demand maximizes the possibilities of ambiguity: signifiers are essentially polyvariant

---

14. Lacan, *Formations of the Unconscious*, 81.
15. Lacan, *Formations of the Unconscious*, 82.
16. Lacan, *Formations of the Unconscious*, 135.

and therefore serve creatively in relation to meaning, evoking the unconscious, if bringing also a touch of the arbitrary.[17] The polyvariance of the signifier is what brings novelty and surprise into language, as expressed in the dreamwork. So, while we don't *need* (in Lacan's sense of the term) to joke, jokes testify to the space of desire (i.e., lack) opened up in the articulation of a need.[18] Hence Lacan's claims that "the sphere of comedy is created by the presence at its centre of a hidden signifier."[19]

Pleasure (the Return)

What then of the question of mirth? "What in witticisms, replaces the failure of desire to be communicated via signifiers, to the point of giving us a kind of happiness?" For Lacan, it comes about in the following way: "the Other confirms that a message has stumbled or failed and, in this very stumbling, recog-

---

17. Lacan, *Formations of the Unconscious*, 76.
18. Lacan, *Formations of the Unconscious*, 103.
19. Jacques Lacan, *The Ethics of Psychoanalysis, 1959–1960*, trans. Dennis Porter (London: Routledge, 1992), 314.

nizes the dimension that lies beyond and where true desire is located, that is, what, because of signifiers, never gets satisfied."[20] Said otherwise, a joke "reproduces the initial pleasure of a satisfied demand even as it accedes to an original novelty."[21] Lacan's point is not simply that the condition of language means we can never say what we mean. Rather, despite the alienation *qua* language one can still reach a mutual appreciation in the negative agreement of comedy, that is, the very semblance of sense in nonsenses. And, inasmuch as a joke provides the condition of satisfaction, it stands for the condition of all satisfaction.[22] In what remains his most succinct definition of the pleasure of a joke, Lacan says "*witz* restores to an essentially unsatisfied demand, its *jouissance*, under the double but identical aspect of surprise and of pleasure: of the pleasure of surprise and the surprise of pleasure."[23]

Drawing on Hegel, one could call this a speculative

20. Lacan, *Formations of the Unconscious*, 135.
21. Lacan, *Formations of the Unconscious*, 87.
22. Lacan, *Formations of the Unconscious*, 135.
23. Lacan, *Formations of the Unconscious*, 121.

account of pleasure in the sense that what constitutes the pleasure is not a sudden agreement of meaning but the coincidence of the lack, which is constitutive of human subjectivity *qua* speech. Or, to put the matter directly in Freudian terms, the mirth of comedy relies on the effect of castration upon the subject.

It is helpful to compare this approach briefly with the evolutionary cognitivist approach to comedy. Robert Hurley and Daniel Dennett's recent study maintains the basic premise of Bergson, that is, that humor corrects a mistaken perception,[24] although it develops the idea within a computation model of the human brain:

> Our brains are engaged full time in real-time (risky) heuristic search, generating presuppositions about what will be experienced next in every domain. This time pressured, unsupervised generation process has necessarily lenient standards and introduces content—not all of which can be properly checked for truth—into our mental spaces. If left unexamined, the inevitable errors in these vestibules of consciousness would ultimately continue on to contaminate our world knowledge store. So there has to be a policy

24. Henri Bergson, *Laughter: An Essay on the Meaning of the Comic*, trans. C. Bretherton and F. Rothwell (Los Angeles: Green Integer, 1999), 15.

> of double checking these candidate's beliefs and surmising, and the discovery and resolution of these at breakneck speed is maintained by a powerful reward system—the feeling of humour; mirth—that must support this activity in competition with all the other things you could be thinking about.[25]

While humor may well be defined in terms of reception, that is, whatever we happen particularly to laugh at, properly speaking "humour is any semantic circumstance (any convergence of contentful elements of a particular time)—exogenous or endogenous—in which we make such a mistake and succeed in discovering it."[26]

In comparing the two approaches (cognitive/psychoanalytic), the issue can be put in the following way: the cognitive claim that jokes restore our perception of veridical reality remains conservative; for Lacan, by contrast, comedy provides an insight into the unconscious and renders comedy the result of the inventiveness of the signifier, structurally reliant on a

---

25. Matthew Hurley, Daniel Dennett, and Reginald B. Adams Jr., *Inside Jokes: Using Humor to Reverse-Engineer the Mind* (Cambridge, MA: MIT Press, 2013), 12–13.
26. Hurley et al., *Inside Jokes*, 117.

coterminous loss/return. It is a point neatly captured in the comic scene from *Duck Soup* when Groucho asks for a number between one and ten. When the response "eleven" is given, it elicits the response "Right!" from Groucho. Comedy, in this sense, signals, as Gherovici and Steinkoler put it, "an ethics of freedom in the idiosyncratic style of one's own desire and the way one answers one's demands."[27]

The Funny Side of Christian Charity: Salmon Mayonnaise

By way of highlighting the significance of Lacan's approach, consider his development of Freud's celebrated example of the "salmon mayonnaise" joke (a relative delicacy in nineteenth-century Vienna). Freud identifies the joke as such on the basis that it evidences the operation of displacement. It is significant because Lacan develops Freud's reading *qua* desire to take the analysis in the direction of Christian charity.

---

27. Patricia Gherovici and Manya Steinkoler, eds., *Lacan, Psychoanalysis, and Comedy* (New York: Cambridge University Press, 2016), 14.

> An impoverished individual borrowed 25 florins from a prosperous acquaintance, with many asseverations of his necessitous circumstances. The very same day his benefactor met him again in a restaurant with a plate of salmon mayonnaise in front of him. The benefactor reproached him: "What? You borrow money from me and then order yourself salmon mayonnaise? Is *that* what you've used my money for?" "I don't understand you," replied the object of the attack; "if I haven't any money I *can't* eat salmon mayonnaise, and if I have some money I *mustn't* eat salmon mayonnaise. Well, then, when *am* I to eat salmon mayonnaise?"[28]

As Lacan says, the joke highlights the relationship between the signifier and desire, and the way that the path of signifier through the intervention of the other shifts the focus and renders ambiguous the demand. The other "profoundly perverts the system of demand" and the response one gives to a demand: "Clothe the naked . . . why not dress the naked men or women in Christian Dior? . . . feed the hungry—why not get them drunk?"[29] Every response to

---

28. Freud, *Jokes,* 49–50. Jimmy Carr provides what amounts to an updated inverted version of this joke: "no matter how much you give money to a homeless person you never get that cup of tea." Jimmy Carr and Lucy Greeves, *The Naked Jape: Uncovering the Hidden World of Jokes* (London: Penguin, 2006), 105.
29. Lacan, *Formations of the Unconscious,* 79.

COMEDY AND TRINITY

a demand falls prey to the signifying complex and sets the scene for the struggle of Christian charity; the other intervenes as a subject, ratifies a message in the code, and renders it more complicated.[30]

To put the matter simply, the beggar requires food as a matter of need and for which a lesser delicacy would serve. However, in the process of articulation (i.e., a demand), desire manifests, transmuting an original need beyond itself. As Lacan says, "[Desire] is produced in the margin between the demand for the satisfaction of needs and the demand for love."[31]

When Freud presents the joke—to which he returns a number of times throughout *Jokes*—he does so initially in the context of a tendentious joke. Tendentious jokes yoke the pleasure of transgressions and take the form of sexual or aggressive jokes along with those that attack institutions and those that attack the very notion of truth.

Taking as its protagonist a *Schnorrer* (Jewish beggar), the salmon mayonnaise joke works through the

---

30. Lacan, *Formations of the Unconscious*, 135–36.
31. Lacan, *Formations of the Unconscious*, 418.

operation of displacement, shifting from the Jewish view of charity to the secular. We laugh at the impertinence of the beggar's demand, but, Freud says, "The truth that lies behind is that the *Schnorrer*, who in his thoughts treats the rich man's money as his own, has actually, according to the sacred ordinances of the Jews, almost a right to make this confusion. . . . The ordinary, middle class view of charity is in conflict here with the religious one."[32]

When Lacan interprets the joke, he does so in a way that extends critically to the notion of charity. His point is that responding to the other is never simply a question of responding to a given need (the secular view) but precisely a question of responding to the desire of the other, that is, that which exceeds a mere need (the theological view). In other words, charity must attend not so much to the immediate needs but to those little object causes that go beyond need and that comedy exploits.

The implication of the above is that both Christianity and psychoanalysis operate in the realm of

---

32. Freud, *Jokes*, 113.

charity and must negotiate the other in the capacity of desire: this is the lesson and the basis of his speculative re-description. Where Freud locates the joke within the classification of tendentious/religious jokes to highlight the distinction between the religious and secular worldviews upon which the joke plays, Lacan problematizes in particular the notion of secular charity to highlight the way in which psychoanalytic practice can speak directly into the practice of Christianity charity, that is, how to respond to the desire of the other.

The Speculative Re-Description of Christianity

Lacan pursues his speculative re-description of Christianity throughout his critical commentary on Freud's *Jokes*. He begins by taking Freud's central insight that a joke presents us with a paradox: on the one hand a joke *is* only to the extent I deem it funny; there is something "irreducibly subjective" about getting a joke.[33] Yet on the other hand, there is a sense in

---

33. Lacan, *Formations of the Unconscious*, 88.

which the pleasure we experience in a joke compels us to seek its authentication in another.[34] Everything comes back to two speaking subjects, hence, "The psychical process of constructing a joke seems not to be completed when the joke occurs to one: something remains over which seeks, by communicating the idea, to bring the unknown process of constructing the joke to a conclusion."[35]

Kierkegaard had already observed that it occurs less to one to laugh when one is alone,[36] and Robert Provine's experiments on the sociality of humor highlight how laughter, as an index of comedy (as opposed to say embarrassment), is thirty times more frequent in social rather than solitary situations.[37] For Lacan, the sociality of humor is such because all demands are, by nature of the signifying function, addressed to an other. The initial formulation of a demand begins in response to another, and therefore

---

34. Lacan, *Formations of the Unconscious*, 93.
35. Freud, *Jokes*, 143.
36. Søren Kierkegaard, *Either/Or*, vol. 2, trans. Walter Lowrie (Princeton: Princeton University Press, 1971), 331.
37. Robert Provine, "Laughing, Tickling, and the Evolution of Speech and Self," *Current Directions in Psychological Science* 13, no. 6 (2004): 215.

all desire must pass through the other, but only insofar as this other is "the correspondent of language and subject to its dialectic."[38]

To underline this point, we can put the issue in the language of deconstruction. The moment of getting a joke equates with a sense presence inasmuch as we fully get the joke, yet this is simultaneously accompanied by a mark of absence that compels us to have that sense of presence confirmed by another (what Lacan calls an "imaginary identification").

It is this moment of "authentication" that allows Lacan to develop further the analogy between psychoanalysis and faith: the authentication we seek in telling a joke speaks to the authentication we seek before God.[39] To be sure, in a move that anticipates the critical reaction to the theological turn within French phenomenology, Lacan warns against any mystical prostration given to the ineffable, invoked through the process of witticisms—a criticism that could be extended to Berger. The moment we attach

---

38. Lacan, *Formations of the Unconscious*, 126.
39. Lacan, *Formations of the Unconscious*, 78.

THEOLOGY, COMEDY, POLITICS

"authenticity" to the mystical position, we succumb to "some ridiculous indulgence."[40] His point might easily be taken as a reductionist critique of religion à la Freud, that is, in the chain of succession, the authentication we ultimately seek is that of the loving and protective father. However, that Lacan pursues the theological analogy suggests that the thrust of criticism lies somewhere else. It is not simply that he is, like so many theologians, critiquing the traditional God of Kantian onto-theology—a sublimity beyond representation, a *noumenal* essence of which we can only grasp the *phenomenal* content. Rather, there is something in the joint articulation of the subject *qua* language that is identified in currents of theological thinking. The distinction he is drawing is not between psychoanalysis and faith; after all, he highlights their synergy. Rather, the distinction pertains to what might be broadly conceived as a Kantian reduction of God to a sublime reference (how the world might be otherwise) to one rooted in the type of

---

40. Lacan, *Formations of the Unconscious*, 137.

ecclesial (i.e., social) foundation that makes jokes possible in the first place.

Indeed, the ecclesial metaphor is explicitly developed by Lacan's subsequent commentary on Freud: "This element of transmission which makes it the case that there is something there that, in a way, is supraindividual, and that is tied by an absolutely undeniable community to everything that has been in preparation since the origins of culture."[41] The community basis (i.e., intersubjectivity) is what makes a joke possible in the first place; that is, in order to make someone laugh you need to have a lot in common. Lacan identifies "community" directly with "*paroisse*," that is, the parish. The subtlety in this term should not be missed, related as it is to *parodia*, that is, parody: "a people who are not from our house, I mean our house here on earth, who are from another world and have their roots in another world, namely Christians, for whom the term appeared within Christianity."[42]

---

41. Lacan, *Formations of the Unconscious*, 106.
42. Lacan, *Formations of the Unconscious*, 107.

THEOLOGY, COMEDY, POLITICS

In short, it is the parish that "shows the limits [within] which a joke will work."[43]

Developing the metaphor further in the direction of the sacramental nature of the church, Lacan goes on to claim that if the parish is the precondition of a joke, then jokes themselves are "the communion wine of speech, ever present and without which we remain empty grails."[44] The implication here is that if a joke relies on the gap or lack that arises between a demand and its articulation *qua* the other, then it accords with the function of the empty grail, the absent center of the parish and constitutive basis of the community. Lacan's point? Jokes are not simply an addition to the language in the way that a metaphor might be considered a mere figure of speech; jokes are the lifeblood of our communities, the absent center around which we coalesce. Jokes, Lacan argues, humanize us in a way that captures the logic of sacramental life. Just as the community of Christians are humanized (i.e., made fully human)

---

43. Lacan, *Formations of the Unconscious*, 108.
44. Lacan, *Formations of the Unconscious*, 107.

paradoxically by virtue of their participation in the Eucharist (i.e., that which is not human), likewise, jokes humanize us by paradoxically starting from what is inhuman (the Other *qua* desire).[45] Hence, as Lacan points out, comedy was historically constituted in the meals offered to the gods through banquets and as Hegel surmised, the aesthetic face of religion.[46]

In sum, Lacan emphasizes the intersubjective nature of comedy *qua* the other in a way that highlights our social dependency *qua* speech. In doing so, Lacan presents a startling comparison between psychoanalysis and Christianity. Comedy, on this reasoning, is not simply a means of light relief; nor is it simply a transgressive moment to restore a given standpoint. Rather, it arises within the practice of what it is to be a community of the Word, and all that the Word entails in the creative impossibilities opened up by desire.

---

45. Lacan, *Formations of the Unconscious*, 107.
46. Lacan, *Formations of the Unconscious*, 121; Hegel, *Phenomenology of Spirit*, trans. A. V. Miller (Oxford: Oxford University Press, 1977), 450–51.

The Comic Drive, or Rather, the *Object a* as the Comic Object

More recently, Alenka Zupančič has developed Lacan's work on comedy from the perspective of the Freudian death drive in a way that foregrounds the "contra-religious thrust" of comedy.[47] One should view her critique of theology in terms of Lacan's, that is, where God is postulated as a *noumenal* essence up against that which runs our human limitations. That being the case, comedy simply reminds us of our human finitude in the face of idealism and encourages the sentiment of tragedy, the opposite of comedy. Neither does she accept the purely materialist outcome. If comedy attests to anything, it is that humans cannot be reduced to the purely material. In other words, we might question the prevailing assumption that comedy belongs to the body: comedy attests to the split between the body and the symbolic.

---

47. Alenka Zupančič, *The Odd One In: On Comedy* (London: MIT Press, 2008), 50.

Drive (as opposed to a biological instinct) emerges as a result of the rupture the symbolic makes with the body; it instantiates itself through that rupture, "as a kind of 'fictional' apparatus in relation to an impossibility that remains lodged at its core."[48] In other words, it structures our relation to the loss of the primary object and the subsequent sense of satisfaction in relation to the lost object. So, while on the one hand our drives are associated with the body, they cannot be reduced to the body as such; they arise in relation to the signifier; although a drive is not a signifier as such, it is produced in the loss of separation and the paradoxical object that Lacan calls *object a*: an invisible and inaudible object that speaks to us through the contours of our desires. As Marie Jaanus puts it, the object of the drive is an "archaic object, annihilating or enticing us from the outside of our being with imminent non-being or the promise of fulfilment."[49]

---

48. Philip Dravers, "The Drive as a Fundamental Concept of Psychoanalysis," London Society, https://tinyurl.com/y894ccvl.
49. Marie Jaanus, "The *Démontage* of the Drive," in *Reading Seminar XI:*

Freud's celebrated example of the "*fort-da*" game highlights what is at stake here. In the example Freud gives, a child throws a bobbin on a piece of string to the accompanying sound "o-o-o-o," which Freud linked to the German *fort* ("gone"). As the child reels in the bobbin, he cries, "*Da*" ("there"). In Freud's interpretation, the game evidences the role of the pleasure principle: it is an attempt by the child to master the anxiety that arises following the absence of the mother through the repeated re-enacting (a pattern to ease cognitive dissonance). For Lacan, by contrast, the bobbin is "not the mother . . . it is a small part of the subject that detaches itself from him while still remaining his, still retained," that is, the *objet petit a*.[50] So, where Freud views the game in terms of mastery and the subsequent reward *qua* pleasure, for Lacan the delight is found in the repetition of the mother's departure as the cause of the split subject.[51] In other

---

Lacan's Four Fundamental Concepts of Psychoanalysis, ed. Richard Feldstein, Bruce Fink, and Marie Jaanus (Albany: SUNY Press, 1995), 125.

50. Jacques Lacan, *The Four Fundamental Concepts of Psychoanalysis,* trans. Alan Sheridan (London: Vintage, 1998), 62.

51. Lacan, *Four Fundamental Concepts of Psychoanalysis,* 63.

words, the pleasure is found precisely in the arbitrary and spontaneous disclosure of the signifying function, with its element of surprise and pleasure. The object marks the point at which language enters the subject from outside and irrevocably shapes the structure of her being, serving as the basis of the unconscious. Properly speaking, then, the death drive is not situated in the realm of biology but the split introduced into the subject by the symbolic. It is not the drive for biological extinction at the expense of our will to survive; it is what drives us to the limit that prevents us ever being able to be reduced to either the merely biological or purely symbolic.

Drive and Pleasure

If drive is more precisely the drive for pleasure, then the structure of the drive and its satisfaction should tell us something of the pleasure found in comedy. Freud postulated the death drive in the light of his observation of repetition, and like the death drive, comedy is also to exploit repetition to comic affect. Monty Python's "Spam" sketch neatly exemplifies the pleasure of repetition when two customers in a greasy spoon café try to order a breakfast from a menu that includes spam in just about every dish.[52]

Unlike desire, for which satisfaction is forever deferred, the drive finds satisfaction not simply in attaining an object or reaching a goal (that is the work of biological instincts); the drive finds satisfaction in repeatedly circulating around the lost object, the object that prevents the drive from reaching its goal: the *object a*. Žižek puts it the following way. Taken from the standpoint of desire, the subject is grounded in the constitutive *lack*, "it exists in so far as it is in search of the missing object-cause." By contrast, taken from the standpoint of the drive, "the subject is grounded in constitutive *surplus*—that is to say, in the excessive presence of some Thing that is inherently 'impossible' and should not be here, in our present reality."[53]

---

52. The use of "spam" in the sketch provides the origins of the email term.
53. Slavoj Žižek, *The Ticklish Subject* (London: Verso, 2000), 304.

Žižek often underlines this conceptual shift with reference to the undead.[54] To say that someone is undead is not the same as saying he or she is alive. The use of "un-" negates our understanding of death while retaining nonetheless the sense that death remains inherent within its dialectical opposite: life. The undead gives voice to the *Real* of life, the mark of the inherent and excessive core from which humanity springs: the death drive.

By way of contrast, consider Bergson's (incongruity) thesis that the moment of comedy is the moment we succumb to the mechanical over and against the *élan vital*.[55] For Lacan and Žižek, it is precisely the *automism* of the drive (i.e., its repetition) that makes us both funny *and* human in the manner aptly described in the joke regarding a patient who having been asked, "Does your family suffer from mental health?" replied "No, I think they quite enjoy it!"

---

54. Slavoj Žižek, *The Parallax View* (Cambridge, MA: MIT Press, 2006), 122.
55. Bergson, *Laughter*, 23.

Žižek's description helps to clarify the "contra-theological" thrust of Zupančič's work. If it is contra-theology, it is so only to the extent that it refuses the classical theological dichotomy of a transcendent source of humanity and our material being (the metaphysical problem of the one and the many). If comedy reminds us of our essentially incarnational being, that is, the materialist standpoint, then Zupančič's point is that the drive and its object testifies to the fact that we cannot be reduced to the material, nor can we claim a transcendent source. As Zupančič argues, the excess of the inhuman over the human testifies to nothing more than the irreducible interplay of material and symbolic interaction, a creation or product of life's own inherent contradiction: "Not only are we not infinite, we are not even finite."[56]

This is Lacan's psychoanalytic twist to Hegel. If Hegelian comedy brings the divine down to the human level, for Lacan the satisfaction found in comedy testifies to the "fact that life slips away, runs off, escapes all those barriers that oppose it,"[57] that is, that

---

56. Zupančič, *Odd One In*, 53.

we cannot simply be reduced to the material level *qua* human. It is not that comedy simply disavows limitations in the comic impetus like Laurel, who remains impervious to the shovel that Hardy lands upon his head with a crashing thump (although that is also the case). Rather, it recognizes the real of human desire such that we can, as Zupančič puts it, make bread appear in the desert.[58]

The Difference between Comedy and Tragedy

At this point we can return to the distinction between tragedy and comedy. When situated within the psychoanalytic framework, we can say that while both are dependent on the principle of incongruity, tragedy and comedy work with the contours of desire and drive, respectively.

Zupančič puts the difference in the following way: tragedy works within the contours of desire (i.e., an unfulfilled sense of lack). Desire is the name for this

---

57. Lacan, *Ethics of Psychoanalysis, 1959–1960*, 314. See also Gherovici and Steinkoler, eds., *Lacan, Psychoanalysis, and Comedy*, 10.
58. Zupančič, *Odd One In*, 218.

sense of difference, and tragedy is the pain of that difference.[59] Take Hegel's understanding of tragedy as an example. Tragedy arises out of the contradiction or tension between the objective circumstance of a given situation (e.g., the law of the *polis*) and the subjective disposition (the law of the *oikos*), two equally valid positions. For Hegel there remains nonetheless a moment of reconciliation within tragic drama inasmuch as the dramatic representation of two irreconcilable yet valid standpoints preclude the audience from taking sides; in this way the audience is spared the one-sidedness of reflection that besets the tragic characters of the drama: contradiction is turned into reconciliation.[60] The pain faced by Antigone voices precisely the legitimacy of both spheres and the necessity to choose. Understandably, then, from the perspective of tragedy, comedy cannot but appear as idealistic, posing neat, reconciliatory conclusions in response to what remains an unsatisfied desire. Yet

---

59. Zupančič, *Odd One In*, 129.
60. Hegel, *Aesthetics: Lectures on Fine Art*, trans. T. M. Knox, 2 vols. (Oxford: Clarendon, 1975), 1199.

comedy, contrary to the dramatic mode, also thrives on things that do not cohere.

Comedy stands at the point of satisfaction, only here the discrepancy is between a demand and its satisfaction, which is experienced as *jouissance* (mirth), surplus satisfaction; that is, the too-muchness of satisfaction. Put in more direct psychoanalytic terms, as Zupančič does, one can say that tragedy stands at the point of demand to the other and is constituted in the manner of a question: "What shall I be for you?"[61] In tragedy, we start with a demand not met. In comedy, we encounter a satisfaction that outstrips the initial demand. Comedy is inaugurated by this surplus satisfaction precisely where it is not expected. Theologically speaking, comedy attests to creation *ex nihilo*, God's spontaneous outpouring of plenitude in the act of creation.

---

61. Zupančič, *Odd One In*, 131.

Christ as *Object* A

Let us return to the *object a*. If in the process of representation, that is, becoming a speaking being, representation inevitably fails (whatever *is* must by necessity become objectified in the very act of representation), then the comic object is never an object as such but located at the level of this remainder (the *object a*): the object of the drive. Hence the comic object is not an object as such, but as Zupančič argues, the truth of the joint articulation is never visible in the given reality yet constitutive of it. This impossible joint is the real comic object, as exemplified in parapraxis such as the Freudian slip: you say one thing and mean your m[o]ther. In comedy we pass imperceptibly between two frames like a mobius strip, with the *object a* serving as the missing link, allowing the discrete transition between two frames; this is the phenomenon that comedy exploits.

Lacan's metapsychology works in a way that outwits classical metaphysical dualism. "There is no encompassing One which holds a structure together—what holds it together is ultimately just the gap of an impossibility language tries to cope with."[62] Like Derrida, he sees life not in terms of a particular instantiation of something universal (there is a Being that is the source of my being) but as caught within a triadic structure that arises from the dialectic of the speaking being. Lacan develops this in terms of the drive, which is shown to be indicative of trinitarian logic inasmuch as it involves a supplement (the *object a*) at the origin. And like Derrida, only more so, he links this directly to Christian accounts of the Trinity.

In *Talking to Brick Walls* (those of the chapel at Sainte-Anne hospital) he turns to the topic of repetition:

> Repetition can only begin with the second time, which turns out to be the one that inaugurates the repetition. If it weren't for the second there would be no first time. This is the story of the O and I. Only, with I, there cannot be any repetition, such that, for there to be repetition . . . there has to be a third [the Other]. This seems to have been noticed in relation to God. He only begins with three. . . . From our point of view as subjects, what might it be for God Himself that can

---

62. Zupančič, *Odd One In*, 41.

begin with three? . . . It is only from three onwards that He is able to believe in Himself.[63]

To explain the above, if, for Lacan, the death drive is the fundamental tendency of the symbolic order to produce repetition in the concatenation of signifiers, then the condition of repetition also relies precisely on the "third" element: the *object a,* the contingent material remainder of the process of symbolization. The death drive gives witness to this virtual object that resists the symbolic form and remains discernible only in terms of the contours of desire, never experienced as such.[64] This is why, to recall Lacan's view of subjectivity, repetition is not simply the repetition of something that cannot be repeated (i.e., the impossibility), but repetition of something that, in the first instance, does not exist in itself.[65]

It is tempting to locate the implications of Lacan within the tradition of negative theology (we can only describe God in terms of what he is not), but the

---

63. Jacques Lacan, *Talking to Brick Walls* (Cambridge: Polity, 2017), 74–76.
64. Slavoj Žižek, *Incontinence of the Void: Economico-Philosophical Spandrels* (Cambridge, MA: MIT Press, 2017), 18.
65. Žižek, *Incontinence of the Void,* 19.

theological implications of Lacan's thought lie elsewhere. The danger arises because in simply negating a given predicate of God in the round of predicates (on the assumption that as creator God can never be adequately described in terms of the objects of creation), the classical God of metaphysics remains curiously intact. By contrast, if, for Lacan, the subject is haunted by something that originates from within, that is, their own impossibility, then the same position holds for God. For Žižek, this is the key to grasping the significance of Christ's cry of dereliction on the cross: man's alienation from God is repeated in God's alienation from himself, and true comedy arises at the coincidence of these frames: the speculative relation that implies an identity of non-identity.[66]

Where does this leave psychoanalysis, comedy, and theology? What if, as Natalija Bonic argues, the aim of psychoanalysis (and by extension politics) is not to bring about a profound transformation in the way the subject perceives the world (the standpoint of Žižek) but to bring about a comic practice that functions

66. Žižek, *Incontinence of the Void*, 35.

through endless repetition and doubling—the aim of which is to allow two mutually exclusive (and under ordinary circumstances, only alternately visible) realities to appear side by side, so as to reveal the gap that unites and separates them,[67] that is, their speculative identity? Indeed, as Gillian Rose argues, comedy is homeopathic: "Suffering can be held by laughter which is neither joyful nor bitter: the loud belly laughter, with unmoved eyes, from North Carolina; the endless sense of the mundane hilarious of one who goes to Mass every day."[68]

The reference to the mass—its endless repetitions, its circularity around the present yet absent body of Christ in the Eucharist (the *object a*), "the communion wine of speech"—is not insignificant here.[69] Lacan directs our sensibility to something of the enjoyment of the mass, not that of a heightened spiritual encounter but the enjoyment of the drive that finds

---

67. Natalija Bonic, "Psychoanalysis and Comedy: The (Im)Possibility of Changing the Socio-Symbolic Order," *Journal of the Circle for Lacanian Ideology Critique* 4 (2011): 106.
68. Gillian Rose, *Love's Work* (London: Chatto & Windus, 1995), 134.
69. Jacques Lacan, *Seminar V: Formations of the Unconscious (1957–1958)*, ed. Jacques-Alain Miller (Cambridge: Polity, 2017), 107.

a satisfaction in the embrace of its failed attempts to attain the *object a*; this would be a liturgical experience of grace that outstrips all our frustrated desire. If liturgy is increasingly the site of politics, then comedy, understood theologically, can also serve as key theo-political practice.

4

Comedy and Politics

Ever since Jacques Derrida divided the opinion of the Cambridge scholars as to whether he should be allowed to go forward to receive an honorary degree on the grounds that his work consisted "in no small part of elaborate jokes and puns,"[1] there has been a disquieting sense that postmodernity spelled the end of serious philosophical and political intent. Terry

1. Barry Smith, letter, *The Times*, May 9, 1992.

THEOLOGY, COMEDY, POLITICS

Eagleton says, "There is perhaps a degree of consensus that the typical postmodernist artifact is playful, self-ironizing, and even schizoid; and that it reacts to the austere autonomy of high modernism by impudently embracing the language of commerce and the commodity."[2]

Yet the place of comedy in our postmodern thought remains unclear, and the issues extend far beyond the parochialism of philosophy. (In the end Derrida was awarded the degree, largely on the basis of votes garnered outside the philosophy faculty.) On the one hand there are a number of theorists for whom our contemporary situation spells the death of comedy: this is the age of comicide in the sense that comic conventions descend into absurdist violence in ways that exceed any earlier historical understanding of the nature and purpose of comedy. Aristotle might have found comedy in ugliness, but he drew the line at comedy causing pain. On the other hand, there is a growing sense that there has never been a greater

---

2. Terry Eagleton, "Awaking from Modernity," *Times Literary Supplement*, February 20, 1987.

pressure within contemporary society to enjoy life and ensure that no stone remains untouched by the comic inflection. Sell-by dates on cartons of orange juice are replaced by the super-ego imperative to "enjoy before," while riotous red inflated Santa Clauses vie among the gardens and rooftops of suburban houses imploring us to enjoy Christmas regardless.

In what follows I want to explore some of the currents of comic theory with regard to the postmodern condition. As I argue, comedy in postmodernity is linked to key cultural shifts within the economic sphere: the advance of capitalism, but capitalism itself might also pertain to the structure of joke. This serves as the basis for rethinking ecclesiology along the basis of jokes and comedy, not in the usual sense that we need to include some light humor within our exercise of church but that the church properly speaking has the structure of a joke, a counter-joke to capitalism.

Comicide

As the title of Erich Segal's *The Death of Comedy* suggests, the story of comedy and its evolution from the classical period (associated with Aristophanes, Plautus, and Menander) through to *Dr. Strangelove* (1964) is best understood as a tragedy to the extent it ends badly. Segal writes from the perspective of the dramatic genre while drawing on the ambiguity of the etymology of comedy: *kōma ōidē*, "the night song," or alternatively *kōmos ōidē*, "the revel song." The Freudian overtones of the "night song" (i.e., dream) should not be missed here. Hence for Segal, "The essential human comedy is an odyssey from estrangement abroad to reunion at home. And the happiest of Happy Endings is . . . laughter in the house."[3]

Aristophanes is the real hero for Segal with *Birds* (414 BCE), proffering the "fullest expression of the comic dream."[4] If *kōmos* focuses on the joys of life

---

3. Erich Segal, *The Death of Comedy* (Cambridge, MA: Harvard University Press, 2001), 26.
4. Segal, *The Death of Comedy*, 85.

in this world—with no regard for the next—as Segal suggests, then the preaching of *contemptus mundi* by the church in the Middle Ages is the first in a line of targeted attacks that have contributed to the overall decline of comedy. The main act in this comicide is given over to Beckett and the *Theatre of the Absurd*: Didi and Gogo will indeed forever wait for their appointment because in the end, there is no ending: "There will be no revel, renewal, or rejuvenation . . . because comedy is dead."[5]

Beckett has replaced Aristophanes's *kōmos* with "tragicomic stasis,"[6] and like *Doctor Strangelove*, we can only hope to muster some vagary of laughter from the prospect of our total and utter destruction, be it nuclear or otherwise.[7] Arguably the real problem, like George Steiner's assessment of tragedy, is that Segal remains too wedded to the dramatic form while extending nonetheless the "death of comedy" as a metaphor for its evolution.

---

5. Segal, *The Death of Comedy*, 452.
6. Segal, *The Death of Comedy*, 451.
7. Segal, *The Death of Comedy*, 454.

Comic enjoyment today certainly seems to tread an increasingly thin line between laughter and lawsuit. It is a point substantiated by the comedian Daniel Tosh who tweeted an apology for including a rape joke in his set in 2012: "There are awful things in the world, but you can still make jokes about them."[8] This is a far cry from the concerns of the nineteenth-century philosophers working in the field of aesthetics, like Hegel, for whom comedy should participate in the supreme task of art: to present a certain idealized image of a free subject.

As Mark Roche argues in his imperious study of Hegel, "If tragedy and comedy are more than just literary structures, a focus on their contemporary fate should bring insight not only into tragedy and comedy but also into today's world."[9] According to Roche, and in contrast to Segal, ours is an age of comedy having passed from an age of tragedy. Yet, like Segal, this is not a happy or reconciliatory state

---

8. Daniel Tosh, tweet, July 10, 2012, 9:57 p.m., @danieltosh.
9. Mark Roche, *Tragedy and Comedy: A Systematic Study and a Critique of Hegel* (Albany: SUNY Press, 1998), 297.

of affairs. The contemporary age gives witness to an ever-increasing corrosion of the public good accompanied by the cultural elevation of individualism, which renders tragedy impossible. If, as Hegel argued, tragedy was an admixture of will and fate played out between the law of the family and the law of the state, then the conditions of postmodernity preclude such a dialectic. Today, individuals reflect not on the social as such but merely "on their private psyches."[10] The postmodern subject remains stuck in a life of self-absorption, unable to transcend the tyranny of one's own intimacy. In a world where "public life is reduced to a merely formal obligation," self-knowledge is treated simply as an end in itself as opposed to the betterment of others.[11] In this sense, the loss of tragedy is allied to the loss of self-sacrifice for others, and the classical admiration that once existed for (potentially tragic) heroes gives way to a comic preoccupation with celebrities where people are known precisely on the basis of their "well-

---

10. Roche, *Tragedy and Comedy*, 297.
11. Roche, *Tragedy and Comedy*, 297.

knownness" rather than any heroic deed. What matters today is success measured by wealth or tweets rather than an ethically driven performance.[12]

If for Roche the outlook for tragedy is not good, neither is it for comedy: "Americans are very fickle about their heroes, and fickleness conduces to comedy, not tragedy."[13] However, "A literary danger of the modern comedy of negation is that the comic heroes' transgressions are so severe as to surpass the limits of the comic: pain and suffering are indeed evident; even murder [or rape] is not beyond the bounds of the modern comedy of negation."[14]

What Roche finds in Hegel's work, by contrast, is a moment of comedy that seems to be lost in much of modern comedy, "a lightness of spirit"[15] in which, like Aristotle, the comic hero suffers no real pain.

Approaching the issue from the perspective of religious studies, Russell Heddendorf's more recent study *From Faith to Fun* argues that the cultural significance

12. Roche, *Tragedy and Comedy*, 299.
13. Roche, *Tragedy and Comedy*, 299.
14. Roche, *Tragedy and Comedy*, 214.
15. Roche, *Tragedy and Comedy*, 213.

of comedy and humor in postmodernity has negatively influenced the culture in ways that have contributed to the loss of traditional meaning within orthodox religions.[16] For Heddendorf the culprit is the postmodern discrediting of rationalism that has led to an increased sense of paradox within culture but also the increased fragmentation and secularization of culture. Under these conditions, fun is understood principally as an "escape from chaffing expectations."[17] His argument is supported more generally by what he discerns as the cultural shift "from restrictive to permissive thinking."[18] Under such conditions, comedy can only degenerate into a purely transgressive act of fun, a secular form of humor that now dominates the cultural landscape. If, as Berger believed, comedy is transcendent in the sense that it allows us to imagine a different state of affairs, then Heddendorf's point is that the secularism of culture can only mean the secularization of comedy,

---

16. Russell Heddendorf, *From Faith to Fun: The Secularism of Humour* (Cambridge: Lutterworth, 2008), xiv.
17. Heddendorf, *From Faith to Fun*, xv.
18. Heddendorf, *From Faith to Fun*, xv.

the loss of its redemptive power, and its reduction to mere entertainment; the eschatological intimation that Berger imbues comedy with cannot hold in the culture at large. Returning to the Bible, Heddendorf nonetheless ends on a note of optimism suggesting that the Bible, understood as comic, offers a redeeming type of laughter, not simply the cultural expression of fun. The task therefore is to debunk modern fun while at the same time defending the transcendence of faith.

We might summarize the concerns of these three accounts of comicide (literary, philosophical, and religious) in terms of the general shift from modernity to postmodernity, which, as I shall argue, can be characterized in terms of the shift from the Oedipal to a post-Oedipal world. What connects the two are broad shifts in the realm of capital, from a production-based economy to a consumer-based economy. If postmodernity means anything, it means consumption now serves as the new social condition: everything is commodified.

Postmodernity and the Post-Oedipal World

As Fredric Jameson famously argued, the experience of postmodernity "correlate[s] the emergence of new features in culture with the emergence of a new type of social life and a new economic order."[19] Jameson charted the shift from market capitalism (associated with the early modern period) through monopoly capitalism (associated with the rise of the nation state) to postmodern, multinational capitalism, which transcends national boundaries. Each shift is linked to a key technological development with the corollary of postmodernism found in the rise of TVs, digital technologies, and advertising. These now become the central focus of economic and social activity. Internet advertising and social media actively mobilize our desires and create ever-new consumer demands.

However, as Jean Baudrillard points out, desire is rarely for an object as such but its sign-value (what it says about us). Objects operate at the level of

---

19. Fredric Jameson, "Postmodernism and Consumer Society," in *Postmodern Culture,* ed. Hal Foster, 111–25 (London: Pluto, 1984), 113.

signification and create new forms of social differentiation (iPhone or Samsung?), which transcend the old categories of class but whose only purpose is to incite further consumer desire to create a new form of economic domination.[20]

Returning to Jameson, where *culture* was a relatively autonomous term (e.g., linked to particular class) giving rise to the distinctions between high and low culture, we now witness a "prodigious expansion of culture throughout the social realm, to the point at which everything in our social life—from economic value and state power to practices and to the very structure of the psyche itself—can be said to have become cultural."[21]

It is not that postmodernism is merely cultural but that the production of culture becomes integral to the production of commodities for consumption to the point that consuming replaces work as the center of life and arbiter of style choice. As Zygmunt Bauman

---

20. Jean Baudrillard, *The Consumer Society: Myths and Structures* (London: Sage, 1998), 49–68.
21. Fredric Jameson, "Postmodernism, or the Cultural Logic of Late Capitalism," *New Left Review* 146 (1984): 87.

puts it, consumption rather than productive activity becomes the focus of life and the integrative bond of society.[22]

Crucially, where pleasure-seeking was traditionally seen as antithetical to work and hence the enemy of capitalist logic—the argument of Max Weber, for whom the Puritan spirit was a deciding factor in the establishment of capitalism—it now becomes the motivating factor.[23] We no longer shop for our basic needs; shopping itself becomes a pure leisure activity.[24]

Writing from a social-psychoanalytic perspective, Todd McGowan puts the issue thus: "The salient feature of contemporary American society is the premium that it places on enjoyment."[25] We have entered the age of the "entertainment economy" and

---

22. Zygmunt Bauman, "Sociological Responses to Postmodernity," *Thesis Eleven* 23 (1989): 46.
23. Max Weber, *The Protestant Ethic and the Spirit of Capitalism* (London: Routledge, 2001), xii.
24. David Lyon, *Postmodernity* (Buckingham: Open University Press, 1994), 57.
25. Todd McGowan, *The End of Dissatisfaction: Jacques Lacan and the Emerging Society of Enjoyment* (New York: SUNY Press, 2004), 1.

with this a new epoch of social relations.[26] Drawing on psychoanalysis, McGowan employs the distinction between a "closed" and "open" world to represent this shift, a shift from a society founded on prohibition of enjoyment to a society that demands enjoyment as a super-ego imperative.[27] Where duty formally implied sacrifice, our duty now is to enjoy.

In the former Oedipal world, one lived with a sense of dissatisfaction at the sacrifice (castration) required even if tempered by the fruits of that sacrifice (socialization). In the post-Oedipal world, there is no area of your life that is not governed by the imperative to enjoy. And this is the point: there is no sacrificial bond (theological or otherwise) that functions to consolidate the social whole anymore; instead, we are condemned merely to enjoy ourselves within our "isolated enclaves."[28] Little wonder that today's society appears to exalt the individual celebrity over and above the success of teams or nations.[29]

---

26. See Michael Wolf, *The Entertainment Economy: How Mega-Media Forces Are Transforming Our Lives* (New York: Three Rivers, 2003).
27. McGowan, *End of Dissatisfaction*, 2.
28. McGowan, *End of Dissatisfaction*, 2.

However, the society of enjoyment has failed in the sense that enjoyment is the one thing that remains inaccessible. "The contemporary imperative to enjoy—the elevation of enjoyment to a social obligation—deprives enjoyment of its marginal status *vis-à-vis* the social order, bringing it within the confines of that order where we can experience it directly and fully."[30] Yet enjoyment, like love, is often only achieved as a byproduct, that is, when we aim directly for it, we miss it; we achieve enjoyment indirectly. As McGowan points out, is this not at its simplest the reason why we wrap presents?[31]

By contrast, the imperative to enjoy creates the inverse condition: the impossibility of enjoyment. Anyone who attempts to enjoy themselves fully will only end up prey to the proliferation of modes of enjoyment. The sense of being unsatisfied provides the motor that propels one indiscriminately to shift from commodity to commodity with a new promise

---

29. McGowan, *End of Dissatisfaction*, 3.
30. McGowan, *End of Dissatisfaction*, 7.
31. McGowan, *End of Dissatisfaction*, 7.

of satisfaction.[32] Under capitalism, satisfaction is refused.

It is a thesis that recalls Lacan's point that the obligation to others enshrined in Kant's moral philosophy finds a curious bedfellow in the Marquis de Sade in a way that is not usually credited.[33] If, as Kant suggested, moral reasoning should be void of all pathological motivations, acting only in terms of respect for the form of moral reasoning (i.e., the categorical imperative), then one can always make the case that Kant's adherence to the law is itself pathological. That is, there is something sadistic about the character of Kantian law, an unconscious dimension to the juridical process that is evident in Sade also: when he inflicts torment on his subjects, he does so out of duty to his own sense of law.[34] In other words, our commitment to the good of the market can quickly become pathological.

---

32. McGowan, *End of Dissatisfaction*, 38.
33. Jacques Lacan, "Kant with Sade," in *Écrits: The First Complete Edition in English*, trans. B. Fink (New York: Norton, 2006), 645–70.
34. "Kant *avec* Sade," Larval Subjects (blog), June 18, 2011, https://tinyurl.com/y9drfmbw.

What lesson should we draw from this? As McGowan points out, if Marxism made the political critique of the economy the major critical lens, the shift from production to consumption and the problematic of enjoyment means that analysis is now best served by the psychoanalytic lens precisely because it takes the problematic of enjoyment as its focus.[35]

Marx and Laughter: Surplus Value and Surplus Enjoyment

Like Hegel, Marx was given on occasion to view comedy and farce as one of the leading principles of history.

> History is thorough and goes through many phases when carrying an old form to the grave. The last phases of a world-historical form is its *comedy*. The gods of Greece, already tragically wounded to death in Aeschylus's tragedy *Prometheus Bound*, had to re-die a comic death in Lucian's *Dialogues*. Why this course of history? So that humanity should part with its past *cheerfully*. This *cheerful* historical destiny is what we vindicate for the political authorities of Germany.[36]

---

35. McGowan, *End of Dissatisfaction*, 3.
36. Karl Marx, "A Contribution to the Critique of Hegel's Philosophy of

Marx is poking fun here at Napoleon and his nephew Louis Napoleon (Napoleon III). However, Marx makes only a single reference to laughter in the whole of *Das Kapital*. It occurs during Marx's exposition of surplus value, according to which an excess of value is produced by exploiting the difference between what a worker is paid (use value) and the value added to the goods produced (exchange value). As Marx explains:

> On the one hand the daily sustenance of labour-power costs only half a day's labour, while on the other hand the very same labour power can remain effective, can work, during the whole day, and consequently the value which its use during one day creates is double what the capitalist pays for that use; this circumstance is a piece of good luck for the buyer, but by no means an injustice towards the seller. Our capitalist foresaw this state of things, and that was the cause of his laughter.[37]

It was Lacan's initial observation of this single reference to laughter that furnished him with the link between the problematic of excess within the eco-

Right," in *Faith in Faithlessness: An Anthology of Atheism*, ed. Dimitrios Roussopoulos, 141–54 (London: Black Rose, 2008), 144.

37. Karl Marx, *Capital,* vol. 1, trans. Ben Fowkes (Middlesex: Penguin, 1976), 301.

nomic apparatus (surplus value being the cause of capitalism's instability) and the excess of pleasure (*jouissance*) produced within the dynamics of the mental apparatus.

As we have seen, Lacan already linked surplus *jouissance* to jokes in the sense that what provokes laughter is precisely the way that speech and language only ever manage a half-saying: desire must always pass through the other. In Marx he discerns a significance to this laughter in the sense that it is revelatory of the exploitative potential of surplus value.[38] Indeed, he goes further: there is a homology between the structure Marx identified and the structure of his own psychoanalytic discourse.[39] Both capitalism and the subject of the unconscious are sustained by an excess that renders the system incomplete, which is the basis for comedy. As Zupančič puts it: "There is something in the status of work (or labour) which is identical to the status of enjoyment, namely, that it

---

38. Jacques Lacan, *Television* (New York: Norton, 1987), 16.
39. Jacques Lacan, *From an Other to the Other (1968–1969)*, trans. Cormac Gallagher, unpublished MS, April 12, 1968, 4.2.

essentially appears as entropy, as loss, or as an unaccounted-for surplus (by product) of signifying operations," that is, the *object a*.[40]

It is an argument developed by Žižek's Lacanian revival of Marxism: the emergent social forms under capitalism can be said to arise historically at the point when surplus enjoyment/lack becomes the social principle as a whole—the superego imperative of capitalism to enjoy, mastering the drive to consume in the endless circulation of commodities.[41] As we become interpolated into capitalism, submitting life to the process of commodification, we are increasingly engaged in the pursuit of an inaccessible enjoyment.

Discourse and Structure

Following the student riots in Paris in 1969, Jacques Lacan attempted to articulate the basic structures of

---

40. Alenka Zupančič, "When Surplus Enjoyment Meets Surplus Value," in *Reflections on Seminar XVII: Jacques Lacan and the Other Side of Psychoanalysis*, ed. J. Clemens and R. Griggs, 155–79 (Durham, NC: Duke University Press, 2006), 162.
41. Slavoj Žižek, *The Sublime Object of Ideology* (London: Verso, 1989), 52.

social relations, what he called "discourse." By "discourse" Lacan means the sets of relations that produce subjective experience, their operative prohibitions, and the subsequent nature of truth and enjoyment that the structures give rise to. Discourse is rooted in speech and the intersubjective nature of life but cannot simply be reduced to speaking as such.[42]

Lacan initially articulated four fundamental modes of discourse (the discourse of the Master, the University, the Hysteric, and the Analyst), the later three being variations on the fundamental discourse of the Master. In the discourse of the Master (which can readily be associated with the Oedipal dynamic), a Master signifier is established and stands in the position of the agent, establishing and formalizing the subsequent field of knowledge. Think for example how the signifier "God" establishes and gives rise to the discipline of theology and without which there would be no theology. Similarly, consider the way a name serves as the locus and primary identification of

---

42. Lacan's seminars of 1969–1970 detail his discussion of the four discourses. See Jacques Lacan, *Le Séminaire XVII: L'envers de la psychanalysis* (Paris: Seuil, 1991).

a person's sense of who they are. However, as subjects are formed in relation to a Master signifier (i.e., law), a negative surplus is produced (the excess of desire: the *object a* giving rise to the unconscious and hence the divided or alienated subject).

The discourse of the Master broadly accords with the "impossible" profession of governance, which Freud identified as one of three impossible professions. The other two are education (i.e., bringing up children) and psychoanalysis.[43] These discourses are impossible in the sense that they produce a subject who must contend with the antagonism of desire and the unconscious. In other words, our traditional social forms were all articulated around the central structure of symbolic castration and hence the failure of any discourse to totalize the social field.

In his later writings however, Lacan introduced a further (fifth) discourse, less a structural variant as it is a new discourse: the discourse of the Capitalist signals for Lacan an entirely new mode of social rela-

---

43. Sigmund Freud, "Analysis Terminable and Interminable," in *Complete Psychological Works,* vol. 23 (London: Hogarth, 1964), 248.

tion—new in the sense that it breaks with the structure of castration. As Lacan says, the discourse of the Capitalist is a mutation of the Master discourse, modifying the entire structure.[44]

The traditional Oedipal dynamic relied on repression giving rise to the unconscious; the identifying mechanism that differentiates the Capitalist discourse is *verwerfung* ("foreclosure"): the rejection of the symbolic of castration. In repression an element is buried in the unconscious; with foreclosure, something is ejected from the unconscious, something that is never integrated into the unconscious.

In the Capitalist discourse, in place of the Master (i.e., the guarantor of meaning) now stands the barred/alienated or split subject who disavows castration and forms relations directly with the objects of consumerism. Capitalism assumes that any given desire is simply a frustrated demand for which a solution must be found, an object to placate the motor of desire; capitalism posits the market as the solution,

---

44. Jacques Lacan, *Lacan in Italia, 1953–1978: En Italia Lacan* (Milan: La Salamanda, 1978), 35.

which provides countless commodities to satisfy desire. As Vanheule puts it in relation to the salmon mayonnaise joke, why the concern, when both can be bought at a price?

By contrast, psychoanalysis entertains desire as a lack, which is then mobilized as the fundamental support of the subject *qua* the unconscious. In other words, the lack, which constitutes desire, can be put to work in psychoanalysis: to become a subject is to become open to the lack that pertains to subjectivity. This is why Lacan considered capitalism more than a discrete issue for psychoanalysis. Psychoanalysis is the reverse side of capitalism.[45]

Foreclosure within the Capitalist discourse does not simply clear the way for unadulterated pleasure (*jouissance*). As Tomšič puts it, "On the contrary, the foreclosure radicalizes the deadlock of *jouissance* and turns the superego into an insatiable demand for jouissance."[46] When everything is framed in terms of grat-

---

45. Stijn Vanheule, "Capitalist Discourse, Subjectivity and Lacanian Psychoanalysis," *Frontiers in Psychology* 7 (2016): 8.
46. Samo Tomšič, *The Capitalist Unconscious: Marx and Lacan* (London: Verso, 2015), 226.

ification of demands, the social bond quickly begins to unravel. Gone are the key questions of existence—"Who am I? What do you want from me? What am I for you?"—which are replaced by market-driven solutions. Why not, for example, take the anxiety out of sex with a sex bot? The question of existence now is not "What do I desire?" but "What should I desire?"[47]

Tomšič helpfully makes the link here to Lacan's claim that if God is dead (i.e., the Master), nothing is permitted.[48] In other words, where there is law and repression, there is always an enjoyment to be had in transgressing the law. But remove the law, kill the father, and he returns as the oppressive super-ego exercising an even greater prohibition. The point is helpfully clarified by Žižek.

> Think of the situation known to most of us from our youth: the unfortunate child who, on Sunday afternoon, has to visit his grandmother instead of being allowed to play with friends. The old-fashioned

---

47. Vanheule, "Capitalist Discourse," 8.
48. Jacques Lacan, *The Formations of the Unconscious: The Seminar of Jacques Lacan, Book 5* (Cambridge: Polity, 2017), 470.

> authoritarian father's message to the reluctant boy would have been: "I don't care how you feel. Just do your duty, go to grandmother and behave there properly!" In this case, the child's predicament is not bad at all: although forced to do something he clearly doesn't want to, he will retain his inner freedom and the ability to (later) rebel against the paternal authority. Much trickier would have been the message of a "postmodern" non-authoritarian father: "You know how much your grandmother loves you! But, nonetheless, I do not want to force you to visit her—go there only if you really want to!" Every child who is not stupid (and as a rule they are definitely not stupid) will immediately recognize the trap of this permissive attitude: beneath the appearance of a free choice there is an even more oppressive demand than the one formulated by the traditional authoritarian father, namely an implicit injunction not only to visit the grandmother, but to do it voluntarily, out of the child's own free will. Such a false free choice is the obscene superego injunction: it deprives the child even of his inner freedom, ordering him not only what to do, but what to want to do.[49]

As Žižek's example highlights, the freedom of the market enterprise brings its own sense of tyranny and anxiety in which inner freedom is lost and for which an answer must be sought.

---

49. Slavoj Žižek, *How to Read Lacan* (London: Granta, 2006), 92–93.

Lacan and Saints

Marx might have identified the laughter of the factory owner with the logic of capitalism, but Lacan puts the issue more succinctly: "Around *surplus enjoyment* there is something like a fundamental *gag*,"[50] or as Tomšič puts it, capitalism is structured like a joke.[51]

In proposing a solution to capitalist discourse, Lacan makes an interesting turn to the figure of the saint, and in particular, the laughter of saints, a counter-laughter to the laughter of the factory owner. Lacan had long considered the parallels between the psychoanalytic establishment and the church. His work anticipates Julia Kristeva's concerted case that psychoanalysis is the last refuge of faith in the sense that they both maintain at their core the practice of charitable love. Lacan frames the relation directly in terms of the figure of a saint:

---

50. Lacan, *From an Other to the Other*, 4.2, italics in original.
51. Tomšič, *Capitalist Unconscious*, 29.

THEOLOGY, COMEDY, POLITICS

A saint's business, to put it clearly, is not *caritas*. Rather, he acts as trash [*dechet*]; his business being *trashitas* [*il decharite*/a pun on transference/trash/charity]. So as to embody what the structure entails, namely allowing the subject, the subject of the unconscious, to take him as the cause of the subject's own desire.

In fact, it is through the abjection of this cause that the subject in question has a chance to be aware of his position, at least within the structure. For the saint, this is not amusing, but I imagine that for a few ears glued to this TV it converges with many of the oddities of the acts of saints.

That it produces an effect of jouissance—who doesn't "get" the meaning [*sens*] along with the pleasure [*joui*]? The saint alone stays mum; fat chance of getting anything out of him. That is really the most amazing thing in the whole business. Amazing for those who approach it without illusions: the saint is the refuse of jouissance.

Sometimes, however, he takes a break, which he's no more content with than anyone else. He comes [*jouit*]. He's no longer working at that point. It's not as if the smart alecks aren't lying in wait hoping to profit from it so as to pump themselves up again. But the saint doesn't give a damn about that, any more than he does about those who consider it to be his just deserts. Which is too sidesplitting.

Because not giving a damn for distributive justice either is where he most often started from.

The saint doesn't really see himself as righteous, which doesn't mean that he has no ethics. The only

> problem for others is that you can't see where it leads him.
>
> I beat my brain against the hope that some like these will reappear. No doubt because I, myself, didn't manage to make it.
>
> The more saints, the more laughter; that's my principle, to wit, the way out of capitalist discourse—which will not constitute progress, if it happens only for some.[52]

Caritas is a complex term in Lacan's work. In his *Seminar VII* on the ethics of psychoanalysis, Lacan associates *caritas* with the order of the good, where the idea of the good is grounded in a broadly Aristotelian understanding of *eudaimonia* ("happiness"). Hence, Lacan's rejection of *caritas* is a rejection of the idea that psychoanalysis should be aiming for the good or happiness of the analysand. As Lacan says, "Doing things in the name of the good, and even more in the name of the good of the other, is far from protecting us . . . from neurosis and its consequences," as evidenced in the salmon mayonnaise joke.[53] By contrast, Lacan frames the ethical stance in terms of desire: "The only thing one can be guilty of

---

52. Lacan, *Television*, 16.

is giving ground relative to one's desire."[54] As Marc de Kesel highlights, the point is not that we act in a way that makes good on our desire (i.e., if you want it, go out and get it).[55] Rather, Lacan's point is that we desire as such, that is, we maintain desire as lack, we desire in a way not circumscribed by neurotic (or in the case of capitalism, in the manner of a fetishist) desire. In this sense, the value of the good for Lacan remains only inasmuch as the good is the price we pay for access to *jouissance*: not in the sense of capitalizing on the loss of the good but passing beyond the limit of the good, moving beyond it to track down the *real* of desire. The ethics of psychoanalysis is characterized precisely by this fidelity to the real of desire rather than the good.

Returning to the quote above, if, as Lacan says, "a saint's business, to put it clearly, is not *caritas*," his point is that the saint does not operate at the level of

---

53. Jacques Lacan, *The Ethics of Psychoanalysis, 1959–1960*, trans. Dennis Porter (London: Routledge, 1992), 319.
54. Lacan, *Ethics of Psychoanalysis*, 321.
55. Marc de Kesel, *Eros and Ethics: Reading Jacques Lacan's Seminar VII* (New York: SUNY Press, 2009), 262.

the good but the level of desire, the very detachment from the good, beyond the good and hence beyond the social: trash (*dechet*). As Tomšič says, the practice of *caritas* mystifies the subject within the structure and thereby highlights that not all suffering is private.[56]

In sum, we need a politics that carries a different logic of humor to that which arises from the contradiction between class. The laughter of the factory owners supports the superiority theory, according to which the owner denigrates the worker. By contrast, the saint's laughter is outside the *caritas* of the market, the standpoint of therapeutic practice and theological critique.

The Joke of Judaism

Christianity has long posed a critical response to the market. Does not Christianity stand for community as opposed to market-driven individualism? Developing Lacan's line of thought, we might ask instead, What if there is something like a fundamental gag

---

56. Samo Tomšič, "Laughter and Capitalism," in *S: Journal of the Jan van Eyck Circle for Lacanian Ideology Critique* 8 (2015): 29.

within Christianity, which arises from the surplus that Christ stands for? To answer this question, I want to return first to its roots in the Jewish tradition. As the name Isaac implies, Judaism was founded in the recognition of a certain type of laughter.

The story of Isaac's naming contains three instances of laughter. To recall, Abraham, having received the news from God that Sarah and he "shall give rise to nations," falls on his face and laughs, saying to himself, "Can a child be born to a man who is a hundred years old? Can Sarah, who is ninety years old, bear a child?" (Gen 17:17–18). This is the first instance of laughter. A little later, while Abraham attends to the three angels under the tree of Mamre, Sarah, who is standing at the tent's entrance, overhears the news. Notwithstanding their advance in years, she is to have a son. Sarah laughs to herself, saying, "After I have grown old, and my husband is old, shall I have pleasure?" (Gen 18:12–13). This is the second instance of laughter. At this point, God asks Abraham, "Why did Sarah laugh, and say 'Shall I indeed bear a child, now that I am old?' Is anything too wonderful for God? At the set time I will return to you, in due season, and Sarah shall have a son" (Gen 18:15). Sarah is then recorded as denying her laughter out of fear, only to be rebuked by God: "Oh yes, you did laugh" (Gen 18:15). Finally, when Abraham reaches a hundred, Isaac is born to him and Sarah, who says, "God has brought me laughter, and everyone who hears about this will laugh with me" (Gen 21:6). This is the third instance of laughter. In what follows I want to draw upon Manya Steinkoler's extraordinary exposition of the piece in the light of comedy and psychoanalysis.[57]

As Steinkoler points out, rabbinical scholarship has tended to draw a distinction between Abraham and Sarah's initial laughter.[58] Abraham's laughter is associated with the joyful reception of the news; by contrast, Sarah's laughter is deemed scornful of God's power. Rabbinic literature has favored the former

---

57. Manya Steinkoler, "Where Babies and Humor Come From," in *Lacan, Psychoanalysis, and Comedy*, ed. Patricia Gherovici and Manya Steinkoler (New York: Cambridge University Press, 2016), 25–35.
58. Steinkoler, "Where Babies and Humor Come From," 30.

type of laughter to the extent that the literature focuses on Abraham's rebuke of Sarah.

For Steinkoler however, one can account for the bias in terms of male anxiety in the face of a sexualized female. The birth of Isaac evidences a complex nexus around sexual reproduction, power, meaning, and transmission in the telling of the Abrahamic covenant, which is specifically related to laughter. And herein lies the twist in the tale: what matters for the success of the genealogy is not the requirements of an all-powerful and all-knowing deity—a God who can make babies—but a castrated God, a God who encounters the limits of his phallic power in a woman, a God whose desire must pass through the other. Sarah's laughter arises in response to the lack in the big Other and is a direct reply to God's incompleteness.[59]

To take matters one step at a time, first, Abraham's castration is already implied by the use of "laughter" in the sense that laughter is the cause of Abraham's fall (a case of what Steinkoler calls "detunescener").[60]

---

59. Steinkoler, "Where Babies and Humor Come From," 26.

God then uses the signifier of Abraham's fall to raise him: laughter becomes the signifier of the promised son. In this sense, Abraham's castration is what makes the comedy possible. Moreover, as Steinkoler points out, significant in this regard is that Isaac is the only patriarch who does not change his name. The fact that Jacob (Isaac's son) is subsequently given the name Israel makes laughter literally the name of the father and links the birth of comedy to the birth of Judaism.[61]

Second, consider again the story. It seems strange that God rebukes Sarah's laughter on the basis that she questions God's power to fulfill his promise when Sarah's laughter is aimed toward her husband Abraham and his ability to satisfy her erotically: Sarah's laughter is directed toward sexual pleasure, not directed toward babies. Sarah's laughter is therefore better understood as an index of Abraham's castration *qua* pleasure; that is, Sarah's laughter is an index of the

---

60. Steinkoler, "Where Babies and Humor Come From," 28.
61. Steinkoler, "Where Babies and Humor Come From," 29.

lack that resides in the other, marking the other's castration.[62]

Third, when God questions Abraham as to why Sarah laughed, asking "Is it because she is too old?," God seems to willfully misrepresent what Sarah says, as if the issue is precisely God's power over childbirth rather than sexual pleasure. Hence Steinkoler's argument that God discloses anxiety in the face of a sexualized female, meeting his limit in the laughter of Sarah. This would account for why her laughter causes God to comment on it twice—first to challenge the reason, second to maintain that it actually occurred: "You did laugh!," as if God himself is not sure. In short, as Steinkoler argues, God's quiet word in Abraham's ear ("Why did Sarah laugh?") amounts to asking Abraham to keep Sarah in line for the sake of peace.[63]

To summarize the above, first, Abraham is castrated before God, falling in laughter, which becomes the index of lack. Second, Abraham is castrated before

---

62. Steinkoler, "Where Babies and Humor Come From," 29.
63. *b. Bava Metzi'a* 87a, https://tinyurl.com/y6vv4mkf.

Sarah in his inability to offer sexual pleasure as opposed to merely procreate. Third, God is castrated before Sarah. In each case the phallic function (i.e., the symbolic authoritative standpoint of the father/master) meets its limits in women, signified by laughter.

After Isaac is born, Sarah invokes the verb "to laugh" (*tsehok*) again: "God has made laughter for me; everyone who hears will laugh over me" (Gen 21:6). What matters for Sarah is not simply the promise of a child who will become the father of a nation but that people will continue to hear the story and laugh in response. In this sense, the laughter, which arises from receiving the joke, *is* the transmission.[64]

In sum, if Judaism is predicated on laughter, we can, following Steinkoler, put the joke in the following way. Yes, you will bear a child and become matriarch to a nation, but you will be ninety, too bent to milk the goat, and suffer the indignation of

---

64. Steinkoler, "Where Babies and Humor Come From," 35.

Hagar.[65] The punchline, however, is to be found in the reception of Sarah's laughter into our own.

How then do we get from Judaism to Christianity? Christian theology has always favored a typological reading of the Hebrew Scriptures, seeking out the figurations of what is to come in Christ in the works of the Old Testament, that is, retroactively reconfiguring the Old Testament in the light of the New Testament. Understood in this way, Jesus Christ is the new Adam, the true Noah, and the second Isaac. In the topographical reading, Christ reconfigures the laughter of Isaac, who now topographically serves as the proto-Christ. For example, St. Clement of Alexandria (c. 150–215 CE) claims: "Isaac . . . is a type of the Lord, a child as a son; for he was the son of Abraham, as Christ the Son of God, and a sacrifice as the Lord, but he was not immolated as the Lord. Isaac only bore the wood of sacrifice, as the Lord the wood of the cross. And he laughed mystically, prophesying that the Lord should fill us with joy."[66]

---

65. Steinkoler, "Where Babies and Humor Come From," 34.
66. Clement of Alexandria, "The Instructor," in *The Sacred Writings of*

COMEDY AND POLITICS

The similarities between typological readings and jokes should not be missed. A joke relies on two signifiers; the second retroactively reconfigures the meaning of a first. But a joke is only ever an instantaneous affair, and a joke does not make Christianity comic as such. For that, it needs to repeat the joke of Christ (the new Isaac). My wager is that this is the task of the church, which properly constitutes Christianity as comic.

Church as Comedy

To help us think specifically about the church *qua* comedy, we can draw upon the distinction between jokes and comedy introduced by Alenka Zupančič. As Zupančič explains, the pleasure of a joke is always found in the instance of getting the joke (it never does to labor the explanation of a joke). While we can pass jokes on to jocular partners to experience again the pleasure, the pleasure itself remains an instantaneous case of what Kierkegaard calls an aesthetic

Clement of Alexandria, vol. 1, trans. Philip Schaff and William Wilson (Schwab, Germany: Jazzybee Verlag, 2012), 74.

pleasure because it evades the categories of time.[67] Comedy, by contrast, is temporal, not in the sense of being a joke that takes a long time to relay but in respect to the way the pleasure is sustained (i.e., the joke's satisfaction). There is a finality with jokes; once we "get it," the veil is lifted, and cognitive function is restored. In comedy, however, the satisfaction arises with an initial joke, and a sequence is constructed that attempts to sustain the initial pleasure through a kind of nonidentical repetition.[68] As Zupančič says, a joke will produce a surprise in its punchline, providing an erratic object sense, which is largely left to die away until something else can fill the space with another joke. Comic sequences do not leave the object sense to die but pick it up, sustaining comedy by making it the basis of a new joke. Comedy, as Zupančič puts it, "is paradoxically continuity that builds, constructs (almost exclusively) with discontinuity; discontinuity

---

67. Alenka Zupančič, *The Odd One In: On Comedy* (London: MIT Press, 2008), 136.
68. Zupančič, *The Odd One In*, 137.

COMEDY AND POLITICS

(the erratic object sense) is the very stuff of comic continuity."[69]

By way of developing Zupančič's work, consider the following sketch by the Two Ronnies, "The Hardware Shop," commonly called "Fork Handles":[70]

> In a hardware shop. Ronnie Corbett (the shopkeeper) is behind the counter wearing a warehouse jacket. He has just finished serving a customer when a new customer (Ronnie Barker) arrives.
>
> CORBETT (muttering—handing a toilet roll to an old lady): There you are. Mind how you go. [The innuendo of "toilet" and "mind how you go," i.e., "go to the toilet," should not be missed here.]
>
> (Ronnie Barker enters the shop, wearing a scruffy tank-top and beanie.)
>
> BARKER: Four candles!
>
> CORBETT: Four candles?
>
> BARKER: Four candles.
>
> (Ronnie Corbett makes for a box and gets out four candles. He places them on the counter.)

---

69. Zupančič, *The Odd One In*, 137.
70. Ronnie Barker, *All I Ever Wrote: The Complete Works* (London: Ebury Press, 2015), 129–31.

BARKER: No, four candles!

CORBETT (confused): Well there you are, four candles!

BARKER: No, fork 'andles! 'andles for forks!

CORBETT (muttering): Fork handles. Thought you said "four candles!"

BARKER: Got any plugs?

CORBETT: Plugs. What kind of plugs?

BARKER: A rubber one—bathroom.

CORBETT (pulling out two different sized bath plugs): What size?

BARKER: Thirteen amp!

CORBETT (muttering): It's electric bathroom plugs, we call them in the trade. Electric bathroom plugs!

BARKER: Saw tips!

CORBETT: Sore tips? (He doesn't know what he means.) What d'you want? Ointment, or something like that?

BARKER: No, saw tips for covering saws.

CORBETT: Oh, haven't got any, haven't got any.

BARKER: Got any Os?

COMEDY AND POLITICS

CORBETT: 'Oes?

BARKER: Os.

CORBETT: (He goes to get a hoe and places it on the counter.)

BARKER: No, Os.

CORBETT: Os, I thought you meant O. (He takes the hoe back and gets a hose.)

BARKER: No, Os.

CORBETT: Oh, you mean panty 'ose, panty 'ose! (He picks up a pair of tights from beside him.)

BARKER: No, no—Os for the gate, Mon repose! Os letter Os!

CORBETT (finally realizing): Letter Os! (Muttering.) You had me going there!

(He climbs up a stepladder, gets a box down, puts the ladder away, takes the box to the counter, and searches through it for letter O.)

BARKER: Got any Ps?

CORBETT (annoyed): For Gawd's sake, why didn' you bleedin' tell me that while I was up there then? (He gets the ladder out again, climbs up, gets the box of letters down again, then puts the ladder away.) Honestly, I've got all this shop, I ain't got any help. (He puts the box on the counter and gets out some letter Ps.) How many d'you want?

BARKER: No! Tins of peas. Three tins of peas!

CORBETT: You're 'avin' me on, ain't ya, yer 'avin' me on? Eh?

BARKER: I'm not!

BARKER: Got any pumps?

CORBETT (getting really fed up): 'and [i.e., hand] pumps, foot pumps? Come on! Foot pumps! (Muttering as he goes down the shop, he sees one, picks it up, and puts the pump down on the counter.)

BARKER: No, pumps fer ya feet! Brown pump, size nine!

CORBETT: You are 'avin' me on, you are definitely 'avin' me on!

BARKER: No, no, I'm not! No.

CORBETT: You are!

BARKER: Washers!

CORBETT (really close to breaking point): What, windscreen washers, car washers, dishwashers, floor washers, back scrubbers, lavatory cleaners? Floor washers?

BARKER: 'Alf inch washers!

CORBETT: Oh, tap washers, tap washers?

CORBETT (grabbing the list from Barker and reading the final item): Oh that does it! That just about does it! I have just about had it! (Calling through to the back.) Mr. Jones! You come out and serve this customer please, I have just about had enough of 'im. (Mr. Jones comes out, and Ronnie Corbett shows him the list.) Look what 'e's got on there! Look what 'e's got on there!

JONES (goes to a drawer with a towel hanging out of it, and opens it): Right! How many would ya like? One or two?

(He removes the towel to reveal the label on the drawer—"Bill hooks"! [i.e., bollocks]!)

In "Fork Handles," we have an initial joke that arises from the ambiguity of Barker's pronunciation—four candles/fork handles. The ambiguity itself thus becomes the possibility for the ensuing comic misapprehension, creating the surplus that is then put to work. The comic sequence rests on the ability to stretch out the initial joke through its nonidentical repetition.

THEOLOGY, COMEDY, POLITICS

The phonetic homology between fork handles/four candles introduces the possibility of another mispronunciation. With the introduction of the "O," the ambiguity between a garden hoe and a letter "O" for a house name sets up the next comic prop—the letter P, or in this case, a tin of peas. The reversal of the referents (a letter for a house name or other object) provides the next quilting point. Note how in the exchange the Master signifier (four candles) is turned into a comic object that our protagonist struggles to gain control over; the ambiguity of the initial object sense then allows further Master signifiers to arise (the letter "O," pumps, etc.), which in turn stretches the comedy out such that it becomes "a singular continuity-through-interruption."[71] A surplus is generated that functions as a cause—or in Lacanian terms, the death drive.

The mastery of the closing punchline—which, like psychoanalysis, requires knowing precisely when to stop—is given by inverting the situation. Rather than us hearing the request in all its semantic ambiguity

---

71. Zupančič, *Odd One In*, 140.

and try to work out the real referent, we are instead told what the final request will be: bill hooks, which we then construct it all its semantic ambiguity and look for the referent at the level of the unconscious: bollocks!

Crucially, it is important that the comic sequence produces a variety of comic objects that are in turn used to further the overall construction of the space rather than released as such.[72] This is why a simple string of gags with no continuity can quickly loose its pleasure; an inner connection must remain between jokes, even as each joke attains a new novelty[73]—what we could call in Hegelian terms a "speculative repetition," that is, the repetition of a non-identity.

If we now translate this theologically, the argument runs as follows. The birth of Judaism was coterminous with laughter, the laughter that arises from the interpretation of God's promise as it passes through the desire of the other (Abraham/Sarah) and gives rise to the joke. God meets his limits in the laughter of Sarah

---

72. Zupančič, *Odd One In*, 147.
73. Zupančič, *Odd One In*, 140.

because Sarah's womanhood challenges God, bringing to the fore the lack in the Other *qua* pleasure: God is castrated.

Christ presents a new typological twist on Judaism. In Christ, God meets his limits in the world, dying on the cross, a kenotic—comic—outpouring that constitutes an excessive event, one that disturbs the traditional symbolic balance. Recall Lacan's theory of the need, demand, and desire, which accounts for the symbolic world. The order of exchange, like the telling of a joke, is based upon the surplus that arises when demands enter the signifying complex: "exchange is based on a constitutive surplus that *eludes* the balance of exchanges."[74] This excess accounts for symbolic castration, the basis of exchange (in the same way that for Freud, the acceptance of the Oedipal law marks a subject's entry into reciprocal social relations). The event of Christ is both the disturbance of the existing order and the condition for the emergence of a new order (the church).

---

74. Slavoj Žižek, *The Metastases of Enjoyment: Six Essays on Woman and Causality* (London: Verso, 1994), 193.

And because Christ stands at the foundation of the church, he remains curiously external to it, occluded by the structure he gives rise to. We cannot grasp Christ directly in his "naked innocence"; he can only be constructed retroactively as the inherent presupposition of the church *qua* symbolic order. In this sense, Christ is the *object a*, "the traumatic kernel 'secreted' by the process of symbolization"[75] and the erratic object sense, which we struggle to gain mastery over—the failure of which produces a surplus that the church puts to work as the cause. If, then, the art of comedy is "a singular continuity-through-interruption,"[76] the church's role is to sustain the comedy of Christ in the above manner. All that remains is to ask, What precisely is the comedy of Christianity?

Comedy and Love

If the *Commedia* of Dante is precisely that, that is, a comedy, it is so because stylistically it ends well

---

75. Žižek, *Metastases of Enjoyment*, 193.
76. Zupančič, *Odd One In*, 140.

with Dante, led by his beloved Beatrice, not so much to a resting point but the eternal difference of love that makes up the Trinity. In this sense the *Commedia* underscores the relation between comedy and love in a way that is taken up by Lacan, for whom "it is not enough, in speaking of love, to be a tragic poet. One must also be a comic poet."[77] To put the matter directly, what if love is structured like a joke?[78] We can build the relationship through six key points.

First, recalling the defining mechanisms that Freud identified in the dreamwork and a joke, love invokes the process of condensation. In love, all of our desires are conflated in the single image of the beloved.

Second, both love and comedy rely equally on the element of surprise and pleasure (or the pleasure of surprise). Love always occurs where it is least expected. Even if the intentionally of two people embarking on a date was to find love, its discovery would not somehow diminish the surprise should it

---

77. Jacques Lacan, *Transference*, trans. Bruce Fink (Cambridge: Polity, 2015), 109.
78. Zupančič, *Odd One In,* 33–34.

blossom. Love yields an uncanniness; hence the eruption of love does not somehow make sense of the world for us. On the contrary, love resides precisely in these unexpected moments, unsettling the lovers, challenging the safety and comfort of our worlds, and throwing those concerned into a discourse made strange. Love is not an answer to prayer or a moment of final reconciliation: "Love is what makes you break down, it is what leads to fiasco."[79] Love is, as Zupančič puts it, an answer to none of our prayers. Little wonder lovers are quick to domesticate the experience as if their love were an answer to a prior demand.[80]

Third, this should make partial sense of Lacan's definition of love: "Love is giving something you don't have to someone who doesn't want it."[81] Love is like receiving the perfect birthday present (which should of course be given in love), that is, something someone didn't know they wanted until they received it.

---

79. Lacan, *Transference*, 106.
80. Lacan, *Transference*, 135.
81. Lacan, *Transference*, 34.

Fourth, it follows from the above that love is reciprocal (in the same way that when one hears a joke, one often wants to tell one in reply). The Lacanian twist is that this reciprocity is based on the relationship between two unconscious knowledges[82]—the perfect example of what Hegel called a speculative relation, that is, the identity of our non-identity.

It is a point neatly highlighted in an episode of *Friends* ("The One with the List"), which underscores the way that love, like comedy, resides in our lack (not as an answer to the lack, but the very lack).[83] Ross remains torn between his current romance with Julie and his affection for his former girlfriend Rachel. His housemate Chandler endeavors to assist Ross with a view to making the choice by suggesting Ross compile a list of both Rachel's and Julie's flaws. When it comes to Rachel, he is quick set out the flaws: she is "spoiled, ditzy, too into her looks, and just a waitress." When it comes to Julie, his only statement is,

---

82. Jacques Lacan, *Encore, On Feminine Sexuality, 1972-1973* (New York: W. W. Norton & Co, 1999), 144.
83. *Friends*, "The One with the List," directed by Mary Kay Place, written by David Crane and Marta Kauffman, November 16, 1995.

"She's not Rachel." Naturally Ross chooses Rachel. In other words, it is because Ross cannot say why he loves Rachel that he chooses her, or rather, his love is founded on something that cannot be given so simply.

One can make an interesting link here with Bruce Fink's insightful commentary of the widow's offering in Mark.[84]

> Jesus sat down opposite the place where the offerings were put and watched the crowd putting their money into the temple treasury. Many rich people threw in large amounts. But a poor widow came and put in two very small copper coins, worth only a few cents. Calling his disciples to him, Jesus said, "Truly I tell you, this poor widow has put more into the treasury than all the others. They all gave out of their wealth; but she, out of her poverty, put in everything—all she had to live on." (Mark 12:41–44)

The offering of the widow (i.e., her love) is not found in giving what she has but precisely in what she does not have. In this sense, her giving is like comedy: it is by virtue of, rather than despite, being castrated.

---

84. Bruce Fink, *Lacan on Love: An Exploration of Lacan's Seminar VIII, Transference* (Cambridge: Polity, 2016).

Unlike Ross, however, the widow's love is not a dark, jealous love. It is, as Lacan would say, "pure and simple . . . it is irresistibly comic."[85] Indeed, is not the widow's offering the Christian counter-joke to Freud's salmon mayonnaise joke?

Fifth, love, like comedy (as opposed to a joke), is dependent not simply on the surprise of the initial event but the ability to sustain the encounter, to make love endure over time and without which the encounter remains precisely that: an amorous encounter. Here the difference between a joke and comedy is informative. If a comic sequence relies, as above, on singular continuity-through-interruption, then love also is the attempt to sustain the field opened up by lack. A joke has a moment of finality after which the pleasure ends abruptly; comedy maintains the suspense through ambiguity. Love is both an interruption, a surprise, and the attempt to sustain that field—not as the mechanical encrusted onto life, but precisely this staccato fluidity comedy gets at, like a pebble made to skip across the water.

---

85. Lacan, *Transference*, 109.

Sixth, as Lacan says, "It takes three to love, not just two"[86]—or rather love, like comedy, requires a trinity. All speech is at some level a request, a call to appease what is lacking within us. However, as Bruce Fink puts it, "What each partner looks for in the other is not necessarily felt by the other to be in him or her."[87] Love, like comedy, plays on precisely that which we do not have: Christ, the *object a* around which both comedy and love circulate and allows us to pass between both heaven and earth.

Conclusion

By way of conclusion, we might return to one of the great mysteries surrounding Jesus: why, notwithstanding any use of irony or puns, Jesus is not recorded as laughing in the Gospels, whereas Jesus is recorded as laughing in the gnostic *Nag Hammadi* texts discovered in 1945. Here, Jesus's laughter abounds. The clue to this laughter recalls the central figure of Isaac.[88] If Isaac serves typologically as a

---

86. Lacan, *Transference*, 132.
87. Fink, *Lacan on Love*, 200.

precursor to Christ (carrying the wood upon which he would be sacrificed), the fact that Isaac is spared serves only to underlie the docetic reading of Christ: Christ's death on the cross was a merely a semblance of the Christ in heaven who indeed does not really suffer. The metaphysical dualism allows Christ to scoff at those below in a divisive laughter: "Simon, bore the cross on his shoulders. Someone else wore the crown of thorns. And I was on high, poking fun at all the excesses of the rulers and the fruit of their error and conceit. I was laughing at their ignorance."[89] Neither are the disciples spared Jesus's humor in other gnostic texts where their ignorance of events becomes the opportunity for Christ to exploit the incongruence for laughter. In the *Secret Book of John*, for example, John is rebuked by a laughing Jesus: "It's not as Moses said 'upon the waters.' Not at all."[90] It is noteworthy that the Docetic tradition presupposes the significance of a God who laughs but

---

88. Guy Stroumsa, "Christ's Laughter: Docetic Origins Reconsidered," *Journal of Early Christian Studies* 12, no. 3 (2004): 267–88.
89. *The Second Treatise of the Great Seth*, in *The Nag Hammadi Scriptures*, ed. and trans. Marvin Meyer (New York: HarperOne, 2007), 480.

can do so only by remaining at the level of metaphysics, that is, by exploiting precisely the contradiction between this world and the transcendent beyond in a way that affirms the thesis of this book: when comedy is engaged from the standpoint of metaphysics, it serves the pathos of *ressentiment* rather than the joy of creation. In other words, paganism produces a comedy born out of rivalry, not love. To return to the question, it is not that Jesus doesn't laugh, it is that we fail to appreciate the central dynamism of trinitarian love directly with the comic, and the task of the church in maintaining love's comedy: the joke that God sets before us, the counter-joke to a world in which laughter is far too often on the side of the capitalist.

---

90. *The Secret Book of John (The Apocryphon of John)*, trans. Stevan Davies, *The Gnostic Society Library* (2005), https://tinyurl.com/yrf387.

Conclusion

Consider the person who, having bought a book on how to avoid disappointment, discovers the pages are blank and promptly orders another copy—an example of an infinite loop. Infinite loops crop up in all sorts of places, like the children's song "There's a Hole in My Bucket." The song's dialogue between Liza and Henry enacts a deadlock situation: to repair to hole in the bucket, Henry must navigate through a process (fetching water to wet the stone to sharpen the axe, etc.) that ultimately requires a bucket without a hole. The last line, "But there's a hole in my bucket," compels Liza to return (*ad infinitum*) to the beginning of the song, "Then mend it dear Henry."

Toward the end of his study on the cognitive dimensions of comedy, Hurley alludes to the experience of an infinite loop within comedy and the cognitive dimensions of comedy. The cyclical nature of infinite loops can give rise to mirth as evidenced by the song, but it can also describe the structure of our neurotic *jouissance*, manifest in the repetition of a symptom. The problem with infinite loops arises when the output of an infinite loop is bigger than its own input, thereby creating a feedback loop, as exemplified by audio feedback. In such cases, the loop will be amplified indefinably until it is broken. The suggestion is that humor might be just the necessary intervention for his type of cycle, that is, that through "humorous transpositions"[1] we might cultivate the positive experience of mirth and break the feedback cycle.

---

1. Matthew Hurley, Daniel Dennett, Reginald B. Adams Jr., *Inside Jokes: Using Humor to Reverse-Engineer the Mind* (Cambridge, MA: MIT Press, 2013), 286.

CONCLUSION

One way to sum up the argument of this book is to say that the discourse of capitalism, which structures our contemporary world, predicated as it is upon desire (i.e., lack), creates its own infinite feedback loop. By turning all desire into a frustrated demand for a commodity, it increases the desire for more and more objects in the ever-vertiginous spin of consumer experience. Like Henry, we become increasingly fraught by the desire to fill the hole in our shopping basket by returning (*ad infinitum*) to the shops.

Another name for an infinite loop is the death drive. The death drive is manifest in our ability to endlessly circle around the *object a* (the proper comic object) in such a way as to transform the failure we encounter in desire (a frustrated demand) into the mirth of non-rivalrous love.

I have also argued that the death drive is one way to describe the church *qua* sacrament, endlessly and parodically circulating around its absent center: Christ as the object cause of desire around which the church ceaselessly revolves, constantly putting to work the

219

surplus of Christ in the transmission of God's initial joke through its nonidentical repetition.

The benefits of laughter to one's general health are well recorded. If my argument is correct, the benefits of a comic reception of a comic God (i.e., the church) and its humorous transpositions within our current climate might also turn out to be salvific for the anxieties of our contemporary consumer age.

Select Bibliography

Amir, Lydia B. "Philosophy's Attitude towards the Comic: A Re-Evaluation." *European Journal of Humour Research* 1, no. 1 (2013): 6–21.

Bakhtin, Mikhail. *Rabelais and His World*. Bloomington: Indiana University Press, 1968.

Cox, Harvey. *Feast of Fools: A Theological Essay on Festivity and Fantasy*. New York: Harper & Row, 1969.

Fink, Bruce. *Lacan on Love: An Exploration of Lacan's Seminar VIII, Transference*. Cambridge: Polity, 2016.

Freud, Sigmund. *Jokes and Their Relation to the Unconscious*, vol. 8, *Complete Psychological Works of Sigmund Freud*. London: Hogarth, 1960.

Gherovici, Patricia, and Manya Steinkoler, eds. *Lacan, Psychoanalysis, and Comedy*. New York: Cambridge University Press, 2016.

Gilhus, Ingvild. *Laughing Gods, Weeping Virgins: Laughter in the History of Religion*. London: Routledge, 1997.

Harris, Max. *Sacred Folly: A New History of the Feast of Fools*. Ithaca, NY: Cornell University Press, 2011.

Heddendorf, Russell. *From Faith to Fun: The Secularism of Humour*. Cambridge: Lutterworth, 2008.

Hokenson, Jan. *The Idea of Comedy: History, Theory, Critique*. Madison, NJ: Fairleigh Dickinson University Press, 2006.

Hurley, Matthew, Daniel Dennett, and Reginald B. Adams Jr. *Inside Jokes: Using Humor to Reverse-Engineer the Mind*. Cambridge, MA: MIT Press, 2013.

Kierkegaard, Søren. *Fear and Trembling*. Edited and translated by Howard Hong and Edna Hong. Princeton: Princeton University Press, 1983.

Lacan, Jacques. *Formations of the Unconscious, 1957–1958*. Translated by Russel Grigg. Cambridge: Polity, 2017.

Leithart, Peter. *Deep Comedy: Trinity, Tragedy, and Hope in Western Literature*. Moscow, ID: Canon, 2006.

McGowan, Todd. *The End of Dissatisfaction: Jacques Lacan*

and the Emerging Society of Enjoyment. New York: SUNY Press, 2004.

Morreall, John, ed. *The Philosophy of Laughter and Humor.* New York: SUNY Press, 1987.

Provine, Robert. *Laughter: A Scientific Investigation.* London: Viking, 2000.

Scott, Nathan, Jr. "The Bias of Comedy and the Narrow Escape into Faith." *The Christian Scholar* 44 (1961): 9–39.

Screech, Michael. *Laughter at the Foot of the Cross.* Chicago: University of Chicago Press, 1997.

Segal, Erich. *The Death of Comedy.* Cambridge, MA: Harvard University Press, 2001.

Steiner, George. *The Death of Tragedy.* London: Faber and Faber, 1961.

Surin, Kenneth, ed. *Christ, Ethics and Tragedy: Essays in Honour of Donald MacKinnon.* Cambridge: Cambridge University Press, 1989.

Tomšič, Samo. *The Capitalist Unconscious: Marx and Lacan.* London: Verso, 2015.

Žižek, Slavoj. *For They Know Not What They Do: Enjoyment as a Political Factor.* 2nd ed. London: Verso, 2002.

Zupančič, Alenka. *The Odd One In: On Comedy.* London: MIT Press, 2008.

Index of Names

Abbinett, Ross, 91
Abelard, Peter, 47
Abraham, 12, 102, 103, 190, 191, 192, 193, 194, 196, 205
Allen, Dave, 1
Ambrose of Milan, 27, 28
Amir, Lydia, 25, 27, 221
Aquinas, Thomas, 27, 28, 29, 120
Aristophanes, 162, 163
Aristotle, 6, 16, 20, 21, 22, 24, 26, 28, 69, 117, 160, 166

Augustine, St., 27, 112, 113

Bakhtin, Mikhail, 18, 35, 37, 38, 39, 40, 45, 48, 49, 59, 81, 82, 120, 221
Baldacchino, John, 92
Baudrillard, Jean, 169, 170
Bauman, Zygmunt, 170, 171
Beckett, Samuel, 9, 163

Berger, Peter, 60, 61, 82, 83, 84, 87, 105, 111, 137, 167, 168
Bergson, Henri, 129, 147
Bonic, Natalija, 155, 156
Brock, Robert, 23

Capito, Wolfgang, 44, 45
Carr, Jimmy, 132
Cazamian, Louis, 32
Chaplin, Charlie, 69
Clement of Alexandria, 26, 196, 197
Cornford, Francis, 39
Cox, Harvey, xv, 18, 50, 61, 82, 83, 84, 87, 111, 221

Dante, Alighieri, 3, 53, 207, 208
Delport, Khegan, 55
De Lubac, Henri, 112
Democritus, 29, 99
Dennett, Daniel, 129, 130, 218, 222
Derrida, Jacques, 106, 114, 153, 159, 160
Dostoyevsky, Fyodor, 52
Dudley, Donald, 25
Dwyer, Ryan, 8

Eckhart, Meister, 65
Eco, Umberto, 16, 30
Erasmus, 17

Fergusson, David, 51
Fink, Bruce, 211, 213, 221
Flieger, Jerry, 123, 124
Fliess, Wilhelm, 121
Francis, Stewart, xv, 46, 49, 83
Frazer, James, 39
Freud, Sigmund, xix, xx, 12, 71, 110, 112, 118, 119, 120, 121, 122, 123, 124, 131, 132, 133, 134, 135, 136,

INDEX OF NAMES

138, 139, 144, 145,
180, 206, 208, 212,
221

Gilhus, Ingvild, 26, 27,
37, 39, 222
Girard, René, 62, 63, 64,
112

Hamann, Johann Georg,
99
Harris, Max, 41, 42, 43,
47, 222
Hauerwas, Stanley, 59
Heddendorf, Russell, 166,
167, 168, 222
Hegel, Georg W. F., 11,
12, 70, 85, 86, 87, 88,
89, 90, 91, 92, 93, 94,
95, 96, 97, 99, 116,
128, 141, 148, 150,
164, 165, 166, 175,
205, 210
Heidegger, Martin, 107
Heraclitus, 29, 99

Herod, 46, 47, 48
Hick, John, 77, 78, 79
Hobbes, Thomas, 33, 34,
35
Hokenson, Jan, 31, 68,
222
Hurely, Robert, 129, 130,
218, 222

Isaac, 13, 190, 192, 193,
195, 196

Jaanus, Marie, 143, 144
Jacobson, Roman, 124
Jacoponi di Todi, 31
Jameson, Fredric, 169,
170

Kant, Immanuel, 5, 11,
12, 26, 55, 70, 72, 73,
74, 75, 76, 77, 78, 79,
81, 82, 84, 85, 86, 88,
89, 97, 101, 107, 138,
174
Kerr, Fergus, 51

Kesel, Marc de, 188
Kieran, Matthew, 23
Kierkegaard, Søren, 11, 12, 70, 98, 99, 100, 101, 102, 104, 105, 106, 113, 136, 197, 222
Kirkland, Scott, xv, 58
Kristeva, Julia, 185

Lacan, Jacques, 12, 114, 116, 117, 118, 119, 120, 124, 125, 126, 127, 128, 130, 131, 132, 133, 134, 135, 136, 137, 138, 139, 140, 141, 142, 143, 144, 147, 148, 149, 153, 154, 155, 156, 174, 176, 177, 178, 179, 180, 181, 182, 183, 185, 187, 188, 189, 206, 208, 209, 210, 212, 213, 222
Lash, Nicholas, 51

Le Goff, Jacques, 30, 31
Leithart, Peter, 54, 106, 107, 108, 109, 110, 111, 112, 113, 222
Lyon, David, 171

MacKinnon, Donald, xvii, xviii, xix, 50, 51, 52, 54, 55, 56, 57, 58, 59, 60, 61, 105, 223
Martin, Jay, 119, 120
Marx, Groucho, 97, 131
Marx, Karl, 12, 54, 175, 176, 177, 185
McFadden, George, 31, 32
McGowan, Todd, 171, 172, 173, 174, 175, 222
Milbank, John, 106
Morreall, John, 33, 77, 111, 120, 121, 223
Moyse, Ashley, xv, 58

Niebuhr, Reinhold, 30

INDEX OF NAMES

O'Connell, Michael, 44, 45, 46, 47, 48
Oecolampadius, Johannes, 44, 45

Parvulescu, Anca, 6
Plato, 19, 20, 21, 22, 23, 67, 70
Pope Innocent III, 41
Provine, Robert, 6, 136, 223

Rabelais, François, 36, 49
Ratzinger, Joseph, 49
Roche, Mark, 164, 166
Rose, Gillian, 86, 89, 91, 92, 156

Sade, Marquis de, 174
Sarah, 190, 191, 192, 193, 194, 195, 196, 205, 206
Scott, Nathan, 59, 60, 81, 222

Screech, Michael, 17, 61, 99, 223
Segal, Eric, 162, 163, 164, 222
Seneca, 29, 99
Shaftsbury, Third Earl of, 33, 34, 35, 99
Shakespeare, William, 52
Socrates, 19, 20, 22, 69, 99,
Sophocles, 51
Stalin, Joseph, 48, 49
Steiner, George, 52, 53, 54, 105, 109, 163, 223
Steinkoler, Manya, 131, 149, 191, 192, 193, 194, 195, 196, 221
Surin, Kenneth, 51, 56, 223

Tomšič, Samo, 182, 183, 185, 189, 223
Tosh, Daniel, 164

Weber, Max, 84, 171

229

Williams, Raymond, 53
Williams, Rowan, xvii, xviii, xix, 51, 53
Wolf, Michael, 172

Žižek, Slavoj, 15, 16, 87, 89, 90, 96, 119, 146, 147, 148, 154, 155, 178, 183, 184, 206, 207, 223

Zupančič, Alenka, 79, 81, 142, 148, 149, 150, 151, 152, 153, 177, 178, 197, 198, 199, 204, 205, 207, 208, 209, 223

Subject Index

big Other, 87, 107, 192
biology, 9, 145

capitalism, xxi, 12, 13,
    161, 169, 171, 174,
    177, 178, 181, 182,
    185, 188, 219
caritas, 186, 187, 188, 189
carnival, 36, 37, 39, 49
castration, 125, 129, 172,
    180, 181, 192, 193,
    194, 206
charity, 131, 133, 134,
    135, 186

Christ, 40, 46, 56, 61, 97,
    98, 99, 110, 152, 190,
    196, 197, 207, 214,
    220
Christianity, 10, 12, 16,
    18, 26, 40, 48, 40, 52,
    53, 54, 65, 81, 95, 98,
    109, 110, 111, 116,
    119, 134, 135, 139,
    141, 189, 190, 196,
    197
church, xxi, 2, 5, 10, 13,
    16, 17, 30, 35, 37, 39,
    40, 50, 80, 99, 140,

161, 163, 185, 197, 206, 207, 215, 219, 220
cognition, 9, 73, 74, 85
corpus Christi, 46
creation, xix, xxi, 60, 110, 112, 151, 155, 215

desire, xviii, xx, 9, 16, 34, 62, 116, 118, 121, 122, 123, 124, 125, 126, 127, 128, 131, 132, 133, 134, 135, 137, 141, 143, 146, 149, 150, 154, 157, 169, 170, 177, 180, 181, 182, 183, 186, 187, 188, 189, 192, 205, 206, 208, 219
dialectics, 26, 88, 89, 90, 95, 96, 137, 147 153, 165
discourse, 177, 178, 179, 180, 181, 182, 185, 187, 209, 219

Divina Commedia, 3, 53, 207, 208
dreamwork, 121, 122, 124, 127, 208
drive, 141, 143, 145, 146, 147, 148, 149, 152, 153, 154, 156, 178, 204, 219

Easter, 44, 47, 49
enjoyment, xix, xx, xxi, 8, 10, 12, 28, 156, 164, 171, 172, 173, 175, 177, 178, 179, 183, 185
eschatology, 111
Eucharist, 141, 156
eutrapelia, 25, 26, 28, 29
excess, 27, 28, 104, 106, 112, 114, 126, 147, 148, 176, 177, 180, 206, 214

SUBJECT INDEX

faith, 46, 99, 103, 104, 105, 106
Feast of Fools, xv, 18, 35, 36, 40, 41, 42, 43, 45, 47, 48, 61, 82
fort-da, 144
freedom, 26, 34, 38, 76, 86, 91, 93, 131, 184

gnostic, 60, 213, 214
God, xix, xx, xxi, 2, 3, 4, 7, 9, 40, 56, 65, 75, 79, 81, 84, 86, 95, 96, 98, 99, 100, 106, 107, 109, 111, 117, 118, 119, 138, 155, 190, 191, 192, 193, 194, 195, 206, 215
gospel, xviii, 7, 56, 57, 58, 60, 62, 63, 97, 213
grace, 47, 112, 157

humor, xix, 5, 20, 28, 32, 34, 35, 36, 38, 39, 44, 106, 129, 130, 136, 161, 167, 189, 214, 218, 220

idealism, 5, 19, 20, 30, 37, 54, 59, 60, 79, 84, 85, 100, 103, 110, 142
incarnation, 7, 56, 57, 60, 81, 98, 99, 148
irony, 24, 25, 57, 99, 213

jester, 48
jouissance, 128, 151, 177, 182, 186, 188, 218
Judaism, 12, 54, 189, 190, 193, 195, 196, 205, 206

kenosis, 7, 56, 60, 61, 64, 65, 95, 97, 206
knight of infinite faith, 100, 103, 104, 105, 106

knight of infinite resignation, 100, 102, 103, 105, 113

laughter, 2, 5, 6, 12, 13, 17, 18, 19, 21, 22, 25, 26, 27, 29, 30, 32, 33, 36, 37, 38, 39, 42, 43, 47, 48, 49, 50, 60, 63, 64, 65, 76, 77, 80, 82, 120, 123, 136, 156, 162, 163, 164, 168, 176, 175, 177, 185, 187, 189, 190, 191, 192, 193, 194, 195, 196, 205, 213, 214, 215, 220
liberalism, 32, 33, 35
liturgy, 40, 41, 42, 43, 157, 210, 211, 212, 213, 215
love, 13, 16, 101, 102, 104, 112, 113, 207, 208, 209

master signifier, 117, 179, 204
materialism, 4, 60, 79, 81, 100, 103
metaphor, 124, 126
metaphysics, 5, 7, 10, 11, 55, 67, 70, 71, 74, 77, 84, 105, 107, 108, 110, 112, 113, 155, 215
metonym, 124
Middle Ages, xxi, 18, 31, 35, 36, 37, 38, 163
mirth, 8, 27, 28, 104, 127, 129, 130, 151, 218, 219

object a, 125, 142, 143, 146, 152, 153, 154, 157, 178, 180, 207

parish, 12, 139, 140
parody, 12, 139
poetry, 26, 93

SUBJECT INDEX

postmodernity, 8, 13, 159, 161, 165, 167, 168, 169
psychoanalysis, xx, xxi, 117, 119, 134, 137, 138, 141, 155, 172, 180, 182, 185, 187, 188, 191, 204

Reformation, 17
religion, 1, 32, 35, 36, 77, 78, 79, 93, 138
repetition, xxi, 144, 145, 146, 147, 153, 154, 156, 198, 203, 205, 218, 220
rhetoric, 24
risus paschalis, 44, 45, 46, 47

saints, 27, 185, 186, 187
salmon mayonnaise, 131, 132, 133, 182, 187, 212

Saturnalia, 39, 40, 45
scapegoat, 61, 64
scholasticism, 29
sin, xviii, 27, 28
Spirit, 87, 92, 93, 96, 98
Stoic, 25, 27, 29, 61
surplus, 146, 151, 175, 176, 177, 178, 180, 185, 190, 203, 204, 206, 207, 200

tragedy, xviii, xix, 7, 19, 20, 23, 50, 51, 53, 54, 55, 56, 57, 58, 59, 60, 61, 62, 63, 65, 68, 69, 70, 94, 97, 105, 142, 149, 150, 151, 162, 163, 164, 165, 166, 175
Trinity, xx, 4, 57, 65, 84, 112, 113, 116, 153, 208, 213

undead, 147